Practical Guide to SAP® Workflow Agent Determination

Gretchen Horn

Thank you for purchasing this book from Espresso Tutorials!

Like a cup of espresso coffee, Espresso Tutorials SAP books are concise and effective. We know that your time is valuable and we deliver information in a succinct and straightforward manner. It only takes our readers a short amount of time to consume SAP concepts. Our books are well recognized in the industry for leveraging tutorial-style instruction and videos to show you step by step how to successfully work with SAP.

Check out our YouTube channel to watch our videos at
https://www.youtube.com/user/EspressoTutorials.

If you are interested in SAP Finance and Controlling, join us at
http://www.fico-forum.com/forum2/
to get your SAP questions answered and contribute to discussions.

Related titles from Espresso Tutorials:

- ► Michal Krawczyk: SAP® SOA Integration – Enterprise Service Monitoring
  http://5077.espresso-tutorials.com
- ► Thomas Stutenbäumer: Practical Guide to ABAP®.
  Part 1: Conceptual Design, Development, Debugging
  http://5121.espresso-tutorials.com
- ► Anurag Barua: First Steps in SAP® Fiori
  http://5126.espresso-tutorials.com
- ► Paul Bakker & Rick Bakker: How to Pass the SAP® ABAP Certification Exam *http://5136.espresso-tutorials.com*
- ► Thomas Stutenbäumer: Practical Guide to ABAP®. Part 2: Performance, Enhancements, Transports *http://5138.espresso-tutorials.com*
- ► Prem Manghnani, Seshu Reddy & Sheshank Vyas: Practical Guide to SAP® OpenUI5 *http://5148.espresso-tutorials.com*
- ► Raquel Seville: SAP® OpenUI5 for Mobile BI and Analytics
  http://5173.espresso-tutorials.com
- ► Robert Burdwell: First Steps for Building SAP®UI5 Mobile Apps
  http://5176.espresso-tutorials.com/

Gretchen Horn
Practical Guide to SAP® Workflow Agent Determination

ISBN:	978-1-71720-348-9
Editor:	Lisa Jackson
Cover Design:	Philip Esch
Cover Photo:	© fotofabrika, #174694587—istockphoto
Interior Book Design:	Johann-Christian Hanke

All rights reserved.

1st Edition 2018, Gleichen

© 2018 by Espresso Tutorials GmbH

URL: *www.espresso-tutorials.com*

Feedback
We greatly appreciate any feedback you may have concerning this book. Please send your feedback via email to: *info@espresso-tutorials.com*.

Table of Contents

Preface

SAP Business Workflow is an incredible cross-application tool for automating business processes. As stated by SAP on the *SAP help portal*, "The main purpose of SAP Business Workflow is to get the right task to the right agent (organizational unit, position, job, or user) at the right time." The workflow definition will define the right work to be performed and will determine the right sequence and time for the work, but how does workflow locate the right people? This book will answer this question by describing the many ways an agent may be defined and determined.

The subject of agent determination is just one component of SAP Business Workflow. I've chosen this as a topic for a book because when the workflow development is finished and the consultant leaves, agent determination is the most dynamic aspect to manage for the people left to support the workflow. This book is intended for workflow administrators who need to support workflows and agents. In addition, it is for workflow developers to equip them with all the available options for defining their workflow definition's agents.

I want to give a special thanks to Rick Bakker, of Hanabi Technology, for his help in reviewing this book.

Introduction

As a workflow administrator supporting a workflow definition, as pertains to agent determination, you will need to have an understanding of how these agents are defined.

As a developer designing a workflow definition, you will not only need to consider all the work that will be performed by the workflow, but also who will be responsible for completing the required work. You will need to have a good understanding of all the aspects of being a workflow administrator; this knowledge will aid you in building easily supported workflows.

This book is intended to be supplemental to the chapters on agent determination and workflow rules from *Practical Workflow for SAP* by Dart et al, 2014, (*Practical Workflow*). Because I am only focusing on one aspect of SAP Business Workflow, agent determination, I have the luxury to go into greater detail with examples and workshops. For some topics, however, I will not repeat what is already so well stated in *Practical Workflow*. For example, in chapter 5 of *Practical Workflow*, Sue Keohan goes into great detail about the SAP organizational structure, whereas in this book, an existing understanding of the HR organization structure is necessary.

Another example: chapter 4 of this book pertains to SAP Business Workplace. This is one place where agents can receive their work items, notifications, and emails. I do not discuss other environments. *Practical Workflow* goes into greater detail listing and describing all the other places agents may receive their work items, e.g. the Universal Worklist, as email via Extended Notifications, or the Business Workflow Workplace to name a few.

We have added a few icons to highlight important information. These include:

Tips	
	Tips highlight information that provides more details about the subject being described and/or additional background information.

Attention	
	Attention notices highlight information that you should be aware of when you go through the examples in this book on your own.

Finally, a note concerning the copyright: all screenshots printed in this book are the copyright of SAP SE. All rights are reserved by SAP SE. Copyright pertains to all SAP images in this publication. For the sake of simplicity, we do not mention this specifically underneath every screen-shot.

1 Workflow agents

Agents are critical for most workflow definitions. Agents perform work for the workflow or they are recipients of notifications triggered by the workflow. This first chapter describes all agent types. Chapter 2 discusses how each agent type is defined.

1.1 Work item recipients

Work item recipients are the agents who get the job done. Much of the workflow processing can be performed by the workflow itself as background tasks executed by WF-BATCH. However, there are times when a human is required to act as an agent for dialog work items. This chapter focuses on how work item recipients are determined. Below are the three agent groups used in conjunction to find the selected work item agents (work item recipients). The groups are possible agents, responsible agents, and excluded agents (see Figure 1.1).

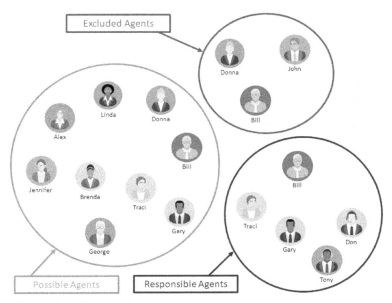

Figure 1.1: The agent groups

Possible agents are assigned to a dialog task. The dialog task will become a work item when a workflow definition instance is created, and its step is reached. The possible agents are a pool of SAP users to be considered to become a work item agent. A user cannot execute the work item if they are not in the possible agent list. Possible agents can be considered fallback agents if no responsible agents are found.

Responsible agents are the agents who are determined at run time from the workflow's step agent definition or the default rule of the task using each workflow's instance-specific data to find the right person. A responsible agent can only process a work item if they are a possible agent and if they are not an excluded agent.

Excluded agents cannot be an agent of the task even if they are listed as a responsible and/or selected agent. Excluded agents are defined in the main workflow as a container element known as an expression.

A user may find themselves in multiple groups (see Figure 1.2):

▶ Donna is in the pool of possible agents, but she is also listed as an excluded agent, so she will not be selected as a work item recipient.

▶ Bill is in the pool of possible agents and in the group of responsible agents, but he will not be an agent because in addition to these, he is also in the excluded agents group.

▶ Jennifer is in the pool of possible agents, but she is not in the group of responsible agents, so she will not be a recipient.

▶ Traci and Gary are both in the pool of possible agents and they are also in the group of responsible agents. Both Traci and Gary are the selected agents (or recipients) of the work item because of this and because neither is in the excluded agents group.

The *selected agents* or *recipients* of the work item are the ones at the intersection of the possible agents and responsible agents and are not included where these intersect with the excluded agents.

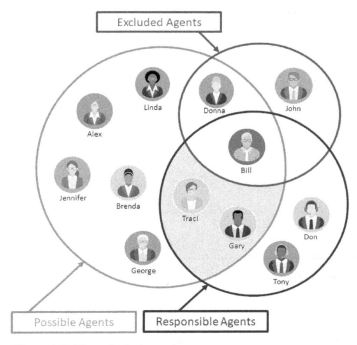

Figure 1.2: The selected agents

Figure 1.2 shows that Traci and Gary are the selected agents, but that is not the end of the story. Who actually completed the work item? This person is known as the *actual agent*. In the example, the actual agent could be Traci or Gary. However, it may be someone else entirely. If neither Gary nor Traci is available for processing this work item, they may have set up substitutes who can process the work item on their behalf. If the substitute completes the work item, then the substitute would be the actual agent. Say that Brenda is a substitute for Gary. Brenda executed and completed the work item, so you can see in Figure 1.3 where the actual agent is recorded as Brenda. You can also see the date/time that the work item was created and how long it took Brenda to process and complete it. Substitutes will be discussed in greater detail in Section 4.3 and Section 6.3.

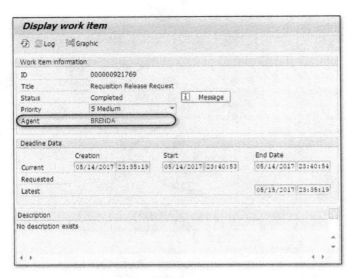

Figure 1.3: Actual agent of a work item

There are many things to consider before you begin defining your agent groups. The first step to finding the recipients of your work item is to define the possible agents. This means you need to identify all the users in the organization who, as part of their work duties, perform the function of the work item. This can be done in several ways and is discussed in the next chapter. However, one of the most popular ways is to assign an organizational object, such as an organizational unit or job. Another very popular way of assigning possible agents is via security roles. It makes a lot of sense to use a security role that would be required for the work that will be performed, e.g. if the task is for approving a customer's credit limit, make the possible agents all the users who have the authorization to actually approve a credit limit.

Secondly, you will define a way for the workflow instance to locate the responsible agents. The responsible agents will most likely be a subset of your possible agents; however, this is not always the case. You need to know all the factors to consider at run time to make this determination. For example, will a purchase requisition be processed differently based on its estimated value? Will an invoice be processed by a different group based on the country where the goods or services were received? And so on. You will need to figure out a way to identify these users within SAP.

Lastly, are there any users who should be excluded from executing the work item? Maybe your workflow will require reviewing the creation or change of a hazardous material in the material master. There may be a group of several employees who create and review these materials. When one employee in the group creates a hazardous material, they should be added to the excluded agents group who approve the work item. By doing this, the employee who created the material will not receive the work item to review/approve it.

Authorization pitfall

 Make sure your selected agents have the appropriate authorization to make a decision in a workflow and then have work performed on their behalf in the background by WF-BATCH.

Consider the following scenario: You have a workflow that seeks approval for purchase order (PO) changes and then updates the PO with the changes if they are approved.

The workflow obtains proposed changes to a PO. A dialog decision task is sent to an agent asking for approval of the changes to be made to the PO. The proposed changes are displayed in the decision task description and the agent clicks, APPROVE PURCHASE ORDER CHANGES. Subsequent to the approval decision step in the workflow is a background step that runs a BAPI to update the PO with the proposed changes. The workflow task points to SAP delivered method BUS2012→CHANGE.

However, in this case, the agent who approved the PO changes does not have sufficient authorization to make changes to the PO. The BAPI changes the PO in the background and all background steps are performed by WF-BATCH. WF-BATCH most likely has SAP_ALL and SAP_NEW (see SAP Note 1251255) and will most likely have the authorization required to make the change to the PO. By coding the workflow this way, a user who does not have authorization to change a PO is still able to make a decision in the workflow that will result in a change to the PO. Note: the purchase order change history will show the change made by WF-BATCH.

You may think that to solve this issue you would simply define the possible agents of the decision step with the role required for changing the PO. However, just because a user can change a PO for plant 1000, does not mean they can change a PO for plant 1010. You might consider defining the possible agents for each of the PO change roles, but this would not work either because the user who can change POs for plant 1000, but not 1010, would be a possible agent because they have the role for changing plant 1000.

One solution is to create a copy of the method BUS2012→CHANGE in a delegated business object, ZBUS2012. Pass the UserID of the agent as a parameter to the new method. Copy the method logic from the original method into your redefined method and you will add an authorization check in the new method before the code you copied.

It might be easier to understand how these agent groups work by looking at a few examples.

1.2 Work item recipient example scenarios

1.2.1 All responsible agents are also possible agents and there are no excluded agents

Say you need to build an accounts payable invoice processing workflow. The invoices will be scanned and an OCR process will detect the vendor's name, among other things. The invoice image and metadata must be routed to the correct AP processing group based on the first letter of the vendor's name. Letters A—J are processed by one AP group, K—O by another, and P—Z by another group. You will define the possible agents on the task as the AP organizational unit as defined by HR. This means that any person or user who is assigned to the AP organizational unit will be evaluated to become a work item recipient. For a person to be a work item recipient, they must have an SAP user ID associated with their personnel record. To define the responsible agents, you build a rule with responsibilities. There will be three responsibilities in the rule, one for each letter grouping. In this case, there are no excluded agents and all the responsible agents are also possible agents. The AP clerks will be assigned to the responsibilities that correspond to the alphabetical groupings as shown in Figure 1.4.

At run time, when an invoice from Kabel Industries comes in, it is scanned into the system and a workflow definition instance is created. The dialog work item for AP processing will be routed to Linda, John, and Don for processing.

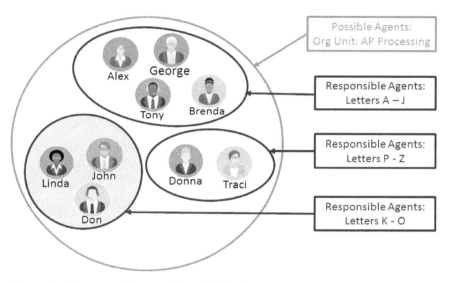

Figure 1.4: Responsible agents by alphabet

1.2.2 Example: Possible agent pool is smaller than what rule returns, no excluded agents

Now, spice up the example a little. The AP processing facility is now global and invoices are being processed in several different languages. The AP processors are now decentralized so they are no longer in one HR organizational unit. You could assign all the AP processing organizational units to the task as possible agents, but you decide to simply assign the AP processing role as the possible agents.

Because the invoices are in multiple languages, it is necessary to consider the language of the invoice when determining the responsible agent. Each invoice must be directed to someone fluent in the language

17

associated with the invoice. You create another rule with responsibilities to accomplish this. There will be a responsibility for each language to be processed. Note: a person may speak more than one language and may be assigned to multiple responsibilities. Additionally, this rule is not exclusive for the workflow; it will be used by other workflow processes in the company so there are many users assigned to responsibilities who are not AP processors.

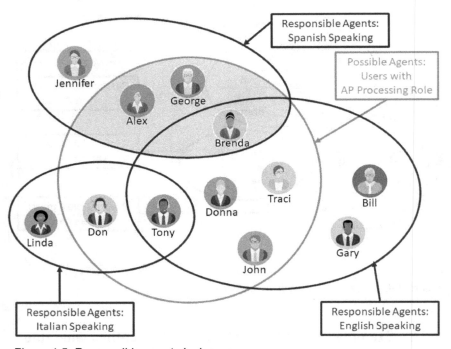

Figure 1.5: Responsible agents by language

Figure 1.5 shows the recipients of the following example: A Spanish invoice is scanned and an AP processing workflow instance is created. The processing dialog work item will be directed to Alex, George, and Brenda. Notice that Jennifer can also speak Spanish, but she will not be a work item recipient because she does not have the AP processor role.

1.2.3   Excluded agent example

To illustrate an agent being excluded, consider the following scenario: A manager wants to reward an employee with a bonus, so they initiate the Immediate Reward workflow and indicate which employee is being evaluated for a reward. All managers in the company have a role that can distinguish them as managers. This role defines the possible agents of the task. There is an HR group of users and a review board that is responsible for approving the reward request. The figure below shows a situation where the manager in the group of responsible users who initiates the immediate reward workflow for an employee is also on the review board. The approval step in the workflow will be defined with an excluded agent as an expression from the workflow container, the workflow initiator, element _WF_INITIATOR.

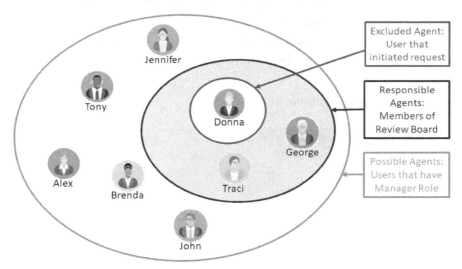

Figure 1.6: Responsible agents excluding excluded agent

Figure 1.6 shows that the review board includes the three users: Donna, Traci, and George. Because Donna initiated the reward request, she is now an excluded agent and cannot approve the request. The request will have to be reviewed by either Traci or George.

1.3 Notification agents

There are some agents who are not responsible for completing the work, but they want to know when the work has been completed or they want to know if the work has not been processed in a timely manner. Below are the events that can have agents assigned, so if the events occur, the appropriate agent(s) can be informed of work item completion or missed deadlines.

- ▶ **Notification of completion**—a work item is completed as expected with no errors

- ▶ **Missed latest start deadline**—a work item has not started on time

- ▶ **Missed requested end deadline**—the first of two events that signal that a work item should have been completed by this time

- ▶ **Missed latest end deadline**—the second of two events that signal a work item should have been completed

Notification of completion

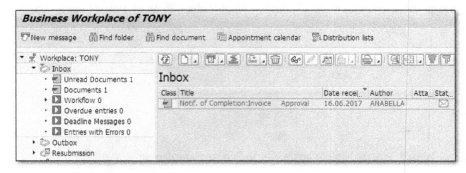

Figure 1.7: Notification of completion received in SAP inbox

Completion notifications are always sent by email to the notification agent's SAP Business Workplace inbox (see Figure 1.7). This notification is sent to an agent upon completion of the dialog work item.

Deadline notifications

The events MISSED LATEST START, MISSED REQUESTED END, and MISSED LATEST END deadlines trigger notifications that are sent as SAP deadline messages (see Figure 1.8). Alternatively, missed deadlines can be defined as MODELED DEADLINES in which case no deadline message will be sent. Modeled deadlines are discussed in the next section.

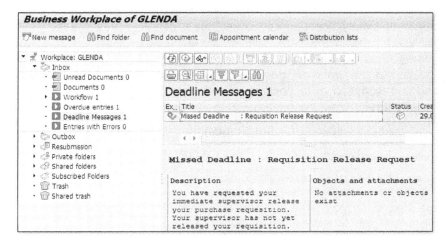

Figure 1.8: Notification of missed deadline

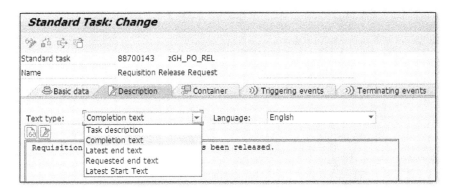

Figure 1.9: Completion and deadline text definition

The notification text is defined in the task definition on the DESCRIPTION tab (see Figure 1.9). There is a dropdown labeled TASK TYPE. It lets you choose the regular task description, completion text, or any of the deadline texts.

1.4 Escalation agents

Instead of simply notifying someone that a deadline was missed, you may want to send the work item to someone other than the selected agent. The action on the deadline step is changed from DISPLAY TEXT to MODELED in the workflow definition. In addition, the new outcome will need a description. It is possible to set up modeled deadlines for the following three of four deadlines.

- ▶ Missed latest start modeled deadline
- ▶ Missed requested end modeled deadline
- ▶ Missed latest end modeled deadline

Note that when you change the action from DISPLAY TEXT as shown in Figure 1.10, to MODELED, as shown in Figure 1.11, the RECIPIENT OF MESSAGE WHEN LATEST END MISSED is removed. This is because the workflow now has a new outcome for handling your exception processing, LATEST END DEADLINE OCCURRED.

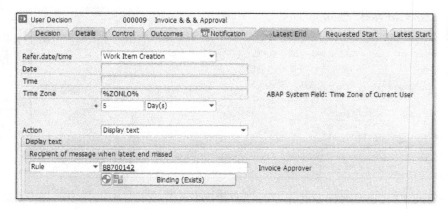

Figure 1.10: Deadline tab set to DISPLAY TEXT

Figure 1.11 shows the LATEST END deadline tab no longer has an agent and the outcome description has been entered as, LATEST END DEADLINE OCCURRED.

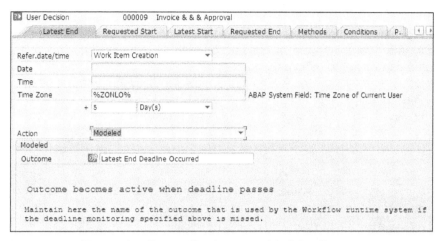

Figure 1.11: Change deadline notification to modeled deadline

This means that you will define a new step in your workflow that will be a normal task and the escalation agent will be defined in the identical manner of defining a task agent. This topic is covered more thoroughly in the workshop in Section 7.3.

Escalation tip

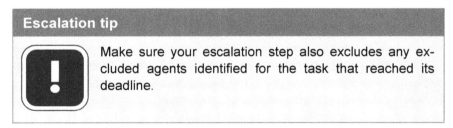

Make sure your escalation step also excludes any excluded agents identified for the task that reached its deadline.

1.5 Deadline timing

Both notification deadlines and modeled deadlines require a mechanism for determining when the deadline(s) occur. The mechanisms available are listed below:

23

▶ Work item creation + offset

▶ Workflow instance creation + offset

▶ Expressions from the workflow container

If you select either WORK ITEM CREATION or WORKFLOW INSTANCE CREA-TION, the event will work in conjunction with an offset value. This offset value can be set to minutes, hours, days, weeks, months, or years. If you select EXPRESSIONS, you will have the most flexibility, but you will need to define container elements for the deadline start date and deadline start time. An alternative to creating container elements is to use virtual attributes or method results.

Incorporate a factory calendar when calculating deadlines

If you would like your deadlines to be based on a factory calendar, you will need to select EXPRESSIONS. You can build your expression by creating a method that calls the function module END_TIME_DETERMINE with the 1) factory calendar, 2) offset value, and 3) start date and start time of either the work item or the workflow instance. Your method will return a structure to the workflow container that contains the deadline date and deadline time.

Time zone tip

Make sure the escalation deadline timing incorporates the time zone where the work will be performed. For example, if you have a critical work item that will go into escalation mode after three hours, the three hours must be counting office/plant hours in the right time zone. If a work item is generated in France at 10:00 AM, for work to be performed on the east coast of the United States; you would need to make sure the three hours begin counting from the work start time for the Eastern Standard Time (EST) zone. If the U.S. plant has the work start time set for 8:00 AM, the work item should escalate at 11:00 AM. If the time zone for deadline monitoring was instead based on the central European summer time zone, the work item would escalate before any agent would have even seen the work item.

2 Agent definition

Now that all the different agent types have been covered, it's time to focus on how each agent type can be defined within the task and workflow definition. Figure 2.1 lists all the agent types and their corresponding definition possibilities.

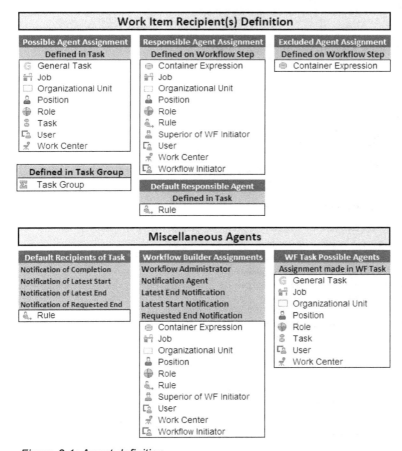

Figure 2.1: Agent definition

Agents belonging to each agent group are defined in different ways. There is quite a bit of flexibility in defining possible agents and responsible agents, whereas the definition of excluded agents is limited to an expression in the workflow container.

2.1 Possible agent definition

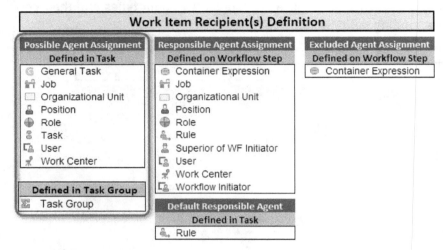

Figure 2.2: Possible agent definition

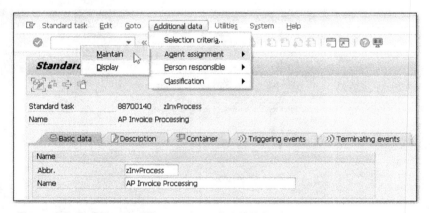

Figure 2.3: Define possible agents on the task

Figure 2.2 shows the ways possible agents can be defined. The possible agents are defined from inside a task, as opposed to being assigned inside the workflow definition (see Figure 2.3). The possible agent assignment does not have access to the task container, and therefore, does not have instance-specific task data available for consideration. The possible agent assignment will be the same for every task instance. The objects assigned to it, however, can be dynamic, in that HR organizational objects are assigned to different users and role assignments are made independent of the workflow. Detailed next are the different ways the possible agents can be defined.

2.1.1   General task

A task may be defined as a general task, which means that every SAP user is a possible agent (see Figure 2.4). It is by far the easiest way to define possible agents, however, the time required for accessing the SAP Business Workplace takes a hit; it must evaluate all the open tasks. If it is a common workflow practice to make all tasks general tasks, there are a lot of tasks that must be read before the user can access their SAP Business Workplace.

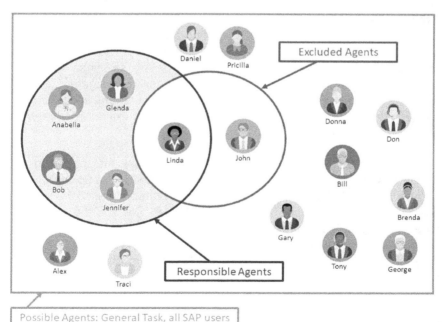

Figure 2.4: General task

General task configuration

 If there are no responsible agents identified, all the possible agents will receive the work item. This makes setting tasks as general tasks dangerous unless you take advantage of T77S0 "WFLOW.ROLE" = X configuration.

Whether your company uses SAP ERP HCM or not, you will have the following organizational objects available for making agent assignments to your task.

- ▶ Organizational unit
- ▶ Job
- ▶ Position
- ▶ Work center

Of course, there is a huge advantage when your organizational structure is maintained by your HR department in SAP. This means that with the new workflow you are rolling out, if you find an organizational unit or job to list as the possible agents, there will be less work to manage. For example, if you decided to use a rule with responsibilities, someone would have to maintain the user and responsibility assignments. Because the HR department is going to maintain the organizational structure, whether or not you have a workflow that uses it, you may as well take advantage of it.

Look at an example where you have a decision task that needs to be sent to customer service agents in central operations. Set up the possible agents in task TS 88700142 with the organizational unit O 50015524 (see Figure 2.5). Figure 2.6 shows transaction PPOM and the organizational unit with the task assigned to it. Another place to make task assignments to organizational objects is from transaction PPOM. By placing your cursor on an organization object and right-clicking on ASSIGN or by clicking on 🔳, you can assign a task here. Instead of having the ability to delete assignments from this transaction, you can delimit the relationship, which is actually a better practice because it will provide a history of the relationship.

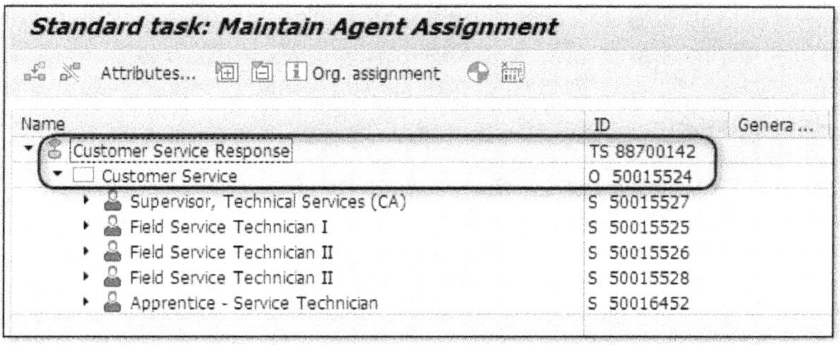

Figure 2.5: Possible agents assigned via organizational unit

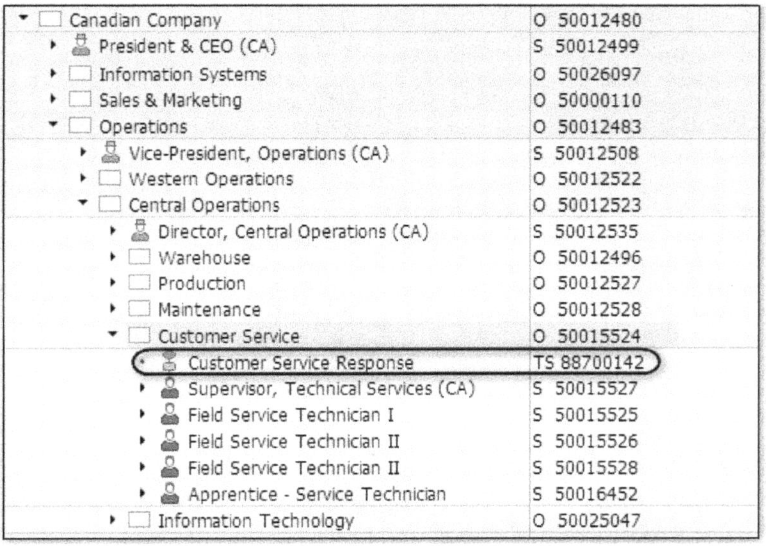

Figure 2.6: T-code PPOM customer service organizational unit

Additionally, you may assign positions as possible agents. This is not usually a good idea, although, it is certainly better to assign a position as a possible agent rather than assigning an SAP user ID directly to the task. This is because as personnel move in and out of the position, the agent determination will not need to change because the position that performs the task did not change, only the holder of the position.

It may make more sense to have your possible agents based on people in the company who have the same job. Figure 2.7 shows how a technician job is assigned to multiple positions across organizational units WESTERN OPERATIONS and CENTRAL OPERATIONS. Figure 2.8 is an example of this job being used to define possible agents of task CUSTOMER SERVICE RESPONSE.

▼ ☐ Operations	O 50012483
▸ 🔱 Vice-President, Operations (CA)	S 50012508
▼ ☐ Western Operations	O 50012522
▸ 🔱 Director, Western Operations (CA)	S 50012534
▸ ☐ Maintenance	O 50012526
▼ ☐ Service	O 50028133
▸ 🔱 Supervisor, Services (CA)	S 50028136
▼ 🔱 Service Technician II (CA)	S 50000605
• 🛠 Technician (CA)	C 50029149
▼ ☐ Central Operations	O 50012523
▸ 🔱 Director, Central Operations (CA)	S 50012535
▼ ☐ Customer Service	O 50015524
• 🔱 Customer Service Response	TS 88700142
▼ 🔱 Supervisor, Technical Services (CA)	S 50015527
• 🛠 Supervisor (CA)	C 50029138
• 🔱 Mr. Jose Ramera	P 00070032
▼ 🔱 Field Service Technician I	S 50015525
• 🛠 Technician (CA)	C 50029149
• 🔱 Mr. George Harowizth	P 00070030
▼ 🔱 Field Service Technician II	S 50015526
• 🛠 Technician (CA)	C 50029149
• 🔱 Mrs Terry Johnson	P 00070031
▼ 🔱 Field Service Technician II	S 50015528
• 🛠 Technician (CA)	C 50029149
• 🔱 Mr. Alex Fieldmann	P 00070033

Figure 2.7: Job—technician

Resolve agents to SAP user ID

SAP Workflow requires agents to be resolved to SAP user IDs. This means that each personnel record assigned to an organizational unit or position must have an SAP user ID assignment made in the COMMUNICATION INFOTYPE, subtype 0001. If your company does not use SAP HCM, SAP user IDs will be assigned directly to the organizational unit, job, or position.

Standard task: Maintain Agent Assignment		

Attributes... Org. assignment

Name	ID	General or Background
▾ Customer Service Response	TS 88700142	
▾ Technician (CA)	C 50029149	
· Service Technician II (CA)	S 50000605	
▸ Field Service Technician I	S 50015525	
▸ Field Service Technician II	S 50015526	
▸ Field Service Technician II	S 50015528	

Figure 2.8: Possible agents assigned via job

2.1.2 SAP system objects

▶ Roles

Roles make the most sense for defining possible agents. You can make sure that the role contains the authorization to complete the workflow task. This will ensure that anyone who receives the work item as an original agent will have the authorization to execute it.

▶ SAP user ID

It is not recommended to set up possible agents as specific SAP user IDs. This is the least-dynamic way to define possible agents and requires the most maintenance.

2.1.3 Tasks

Assignments via tasks is older functionality that is rarely used. If you select it, it is similar to a task group bringing in agents, but you can only use T tasks (customer tasks), as opposed to TS tasks (standard tasks).

2.1.4 Task group

Task groups provide a great way to group tasks that will all have the same agents. Take a look at an example of some auditing tasks. Figure 2.9 is the definition of a task group used for multiple auditing tasks. The auditing tasks were added to the STANDARD TASK tab. To maintain the possible agents for the task group, from the task group definition go to EXTRAS • AGENT ASSIGNMENT • MAINTAIN (see Figure 2.10).

Figure 2.9: Task group definition

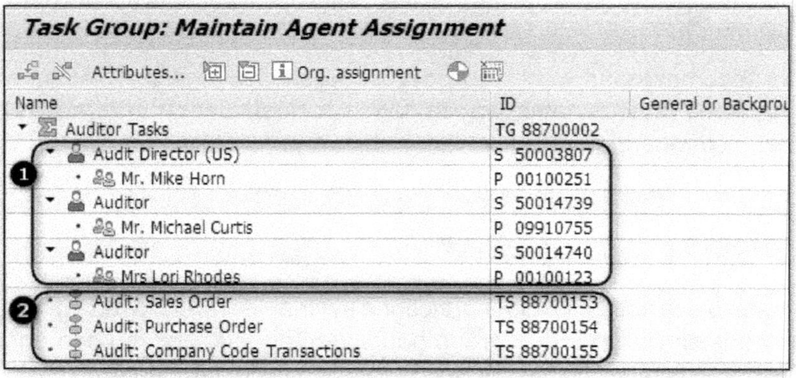

Figure 2.10: Task group possible agent assignment

❶ in Figure 2.10 shows the three auditor positions assigned to the task group. ❷ in Figure 2.10 shows the three tasks that were assigned to the task group on the STANDARD TASKS tab. They automatically show up where agent assignment is maintained.

By maintaining the task group and making the auditors the possible agents for the task group, you have completed the possible agent assignment on all three of the auditor tasks. See an example auditor task in Figure 2.11 which shows the auditors assigned under the task group umbrella. The task group allows you to make changes in just one place, the task group, instead of setting up possible agents individually in the three tasks. This not only saves times, but helps ensure accuracy.

Standard task: Maintain Agent Assignment

⚄ ⚅ Attributes... 🔲 🔳 ⓘ Org. assignment 🔵 🔲

Name	ID	General or Background Task
▼ 🔲 Audit: Company Code Transactions	TS 88700155	
▼ 📚 Auditor Tasks	TG 88700002	
▸ 👤 Audit Director (US)	S 50003807	
▸ 👤 Auditor	S 50014739	
▸ 👤 Auditor	S 50014740	

Figure 2.11: Task of task group agent assignment

2.2   Responsible agent definition

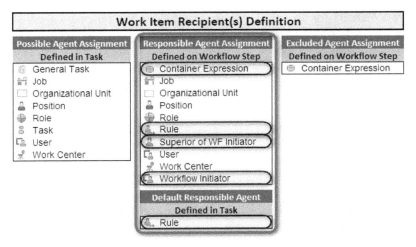

Figure 2.12: Responsible agent definition options

Unlike possible agent assignment, which is a general pool of users who can execute the task, responsible agents are determined using runtime information. For example, all purchase requisition approvers may be defined as users who have a particular role, and may in turn be defined as the possible agents, but it isn't until runtime that you know the cost center assigned to a requisition. The cost center, in the example, is what directs the requisition to the actual approver, who is in the pool of responsible agents.

All the ways that agents are defined as possible agents, except one, are available for defining responsible agents. The one exception is the general task.

Figure 2.12 lists all the ways that a responsible agent may be defined. The circled items are available for defining responsible agents, but not available for defining possible agents. The items that are not circled were already defined in the preceding section where possible agent types were defined.

2.2.1   Expression in workflow container

An *expression* in a workflow container is simply a container element. For an expression to be used as an agent it should be the same type as the structure WFSYST for field INITIATOR. This field is the concatenation of the one- or two-character organizational type, e.g. US for user, S for position, C for work center, and then the organizational ID. If the organizational type is one character, then there must be a space between the organizational type and the organizational ID. This expression can be a single entry or it may be multiline.

Save a background process

For BOR objects, create a virtual attribute for your agent(s) with WFSYST-INITIATOR; or for a BOR object or an ABAP class, create a result method to find your agent(s). This way you can call the method or use the virtual attribute in your workflow via task binding or you can use a container operation without having to call a method in the background to obtain the agent(s).

2.2.2 Workflow rules

Workflow rules combine logic and runtime information to obtain workflow agents. If you select a rule to find your responsible agent, you will need to bind the workflow container elements to the rule container. Using a rule gives automatic functionality for causing an error if no agent is found. For complete information on workflow rules, see Chapter 3.

2.2.3 Superior of workflow initiator

If you select the SUPERIOR OF WORKFLOW INITIATOR, the RULE 00000168 will be inserted. The workflow initiator will be automatically bound to the rule's container element ORG_OBJECT (see Figure 2.13). Of course, the workflow initiator can be replaced with any user you want to find the superior of. This rule determines the organizational unit of the user assigned to ORG_OBJECT and then finds the head of this organizational unit and this person becomes the task's agent.

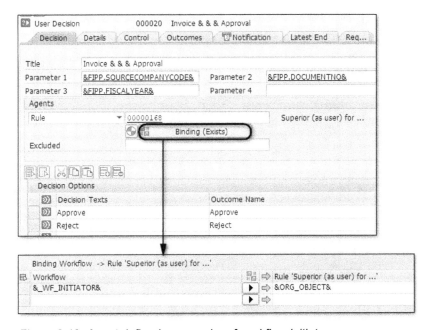

Figure 2.13: Agent defined as superior of workflow initiator

2.2.4 Workflow initiator

The workflow initiator is a container element, also known as an expression. The workflow initiator is a single field of type WFSYST-INITIATOR. This field will contain the value US for the organizational type of user, concatenated with the user ID of the person that initiated the workflow. There are many ways a workflow can be started. For instance, the workflow initiator may have directly started the workflow from generic object services (GOS) or they may have processed something in SAP that caused an event to begin the workflow.

2.2.5 Default rule

Responsible agents can be defined from inside the task using a default rule. The binding for this rule's container elements come from the task container. A task can stand alone as a single-step task. This means there is no workflow definition calling the task. If there is no workflow definition, the only way to define recipients is by combining the default rule with the possible agents.

2.3 Excluded agent definition

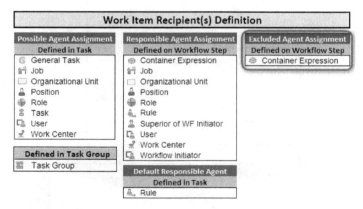

Figure 2.14: Excluded agent definition

The excluded agent is defined in one way, as a workflow container expression, see Figure 2.14. It may be a single or multiline element. The expression may be an attribute of an object, a method result, or it can be an individual element. Individual elements can be populated from a method via binding or a container operation. Often, the actual agent from a preceding task will be appended to an excluded agent container element (see Figure 2.15).

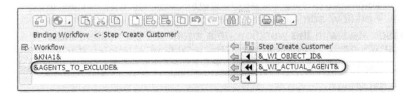

Figure 2.15: Bind actual agent to workflow expression

Workflow administrator can be an excluded agent

 The workflow administrator, even if they are an excluded agent, can execute the work item. The workflow log contains an audit trail noting that the work item was executed by the administrator.

2.4 Miscellaneous agents

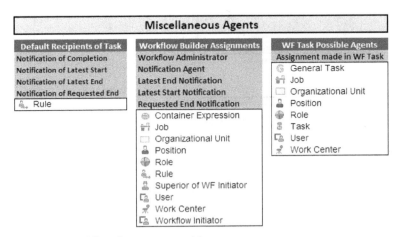

Figure 2.16: Miscellaneous agent types

There are additional agents who can be defined in a workflow definition.

▶ Workflow administrator

A workflow administrator can be set at the workflow level for a single workflow definition. If assigned at the workflow level, this will supersede the global workflow administrator defined via t-code SWU3. If there are errors associated with the workflow, this agent will be notified instead of the global workflow administrator. The workflow administrator can be defined using the same techniques afforded to the responsible agents, found in Section 2.2.

▶ Default notification agents

These agents are defined in the task, transaction PFTC, and must be defined as a rule. The rule will have binding to the task container as opposed to the workflow container. Figure 2.17 shows the four default notification agents.

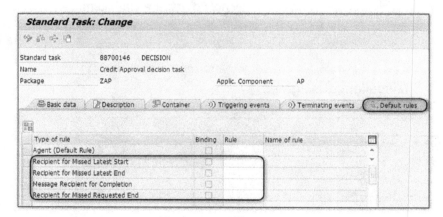

Figure 2.17: Default notification agents in task

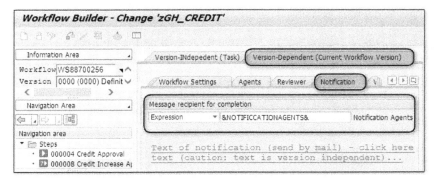

Figure 2.18: Completion notification agent

▶ Deadline notification agents

Deadline notification agents (LATEST START, LATEST END, and REQUESTED END) are defined with all the flexibility as a responsible agent, see Figure 2.19. Note there is no notification agent for the requested start deadline.

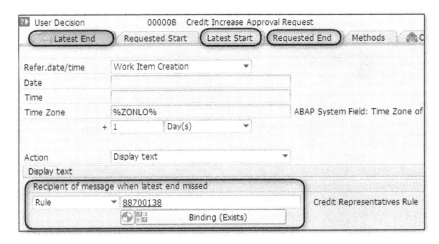

Figure 2.19: Workflow deadline notification agents

► Workflow task possible agents

Define possible agents for your workflow task if you want your agents to start the workflow manually from GOS. The workflow task possible agents are defined in the same way possible agents are assigned to standard task. See Figure 2.20 for an example of a user starting a workflow from inside a requisition. This requisition requires release and the workflow will seek this approval for release.

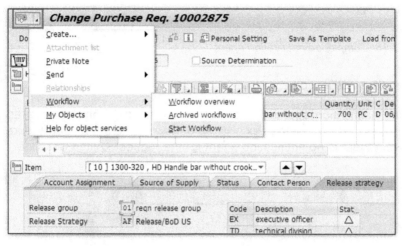

Figure 2.20: Start workflow from generic object services (GOS)

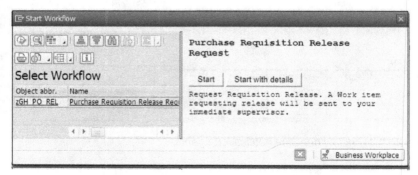

Figure 2.21: Possible workflows for user to start

Figure 2.21 shows the list of workflows that the user is authorized to start. In this case, because the user is in a requisition transaction, this is a list of all the workflows that have the business object BUS2105 in the workflow container and have this user as a possible workflow task agent. Note, the requisition document type determines which business object will be referenced. If the user is in a requisition that has overall release, they will only see workflows associated with overall release. If the user is inside a requisition that has item-level release, they will see workflows associated with item-level release. When the requisition type is configured there is a flag, OvRelPReq that is checked for header-level releases and not checked for item-level releases. Business Object BUS2015 is utilized for header-level releases. Business Object BUS2019 is utilized for item-level releases.

The user is a possible agent of the workflow task because they are assigned the necessary role, see Figure 2.22. All users possessing this role can start this workflow.

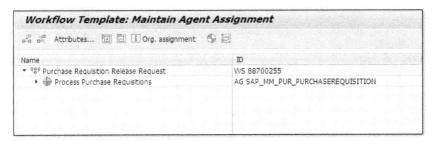

Figure 2.22: Workflow task agent assignment

3 Workflow rules

A workflow rule is just one of the multiple ways to define an agent, but it deserves its own chapter because there are many ways to define rules. A workflow rule is the most flexible definition type available. Workflow rules are created via transaction PFAC.

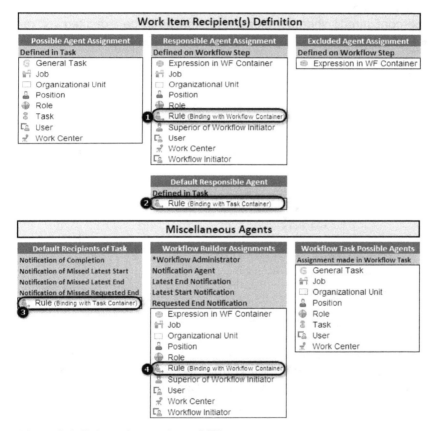

Figure 3.1: Rule assignment possibilities

Workflow rules are used to determine agents in multiple areas. Figure 3.1 shows all the places where a rule can be assigned. A rule can be used to find the responsible agent(s), both from the task as a default rule

❷ and from the workflow where the main agent assignment is made ❶. In addition, rules are used to define default notification recipients (completion, missed latest start, etc.) from within the task ❸. Rules can be used inside the workflow definition to define the deadline and notification agents ❹. Finally, a rule can be used to define a workflow-specific administrator. If a workflow administrator is defined in the workflow, then this will override the system-defined workflow administrator.

There are many types, or categories, of rules that can be defined. This chapter focuses on the categories indicated in Figure 3.2. Some rules can be configured, whereas rules with functions to be executed will require ABAP knowledge.

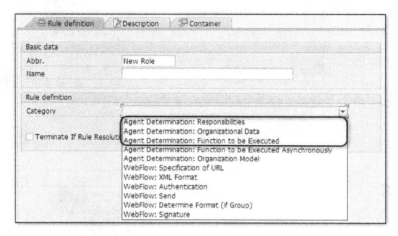

Figure 3.2: Rule categories

One nice thing about a rule is that you can decide to terminate a workflow instance in an error status if no agent is found. See Figure 3.3. This will trigger an email that will be sent to the workflow administrator. The workflow administrator can then correct the agent rules and then re-execute the agent rules for the work item. See Section 6.1.3.

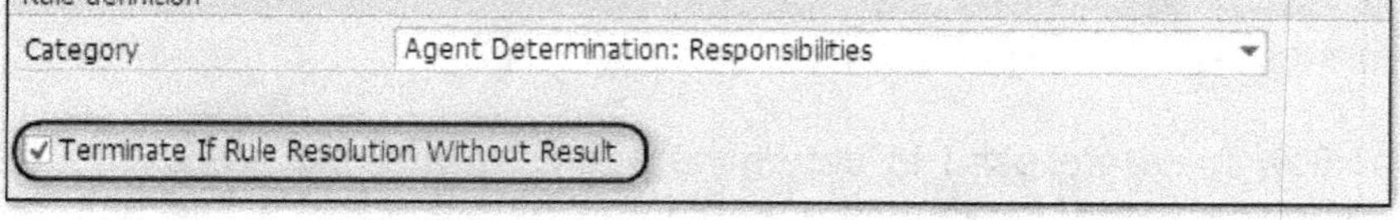

Figure 3.3: Terminate rule if no agent is found

Each rule, with the exception of rules that read organizational data, as shown in Section 3.4, will have a container. There is a CONTAINER tab on the rule definition (see Figure 3.4). The rule container will hold any number of elements that are populated via binding from the workflow container at run time.

Figure 3.4: Rule container

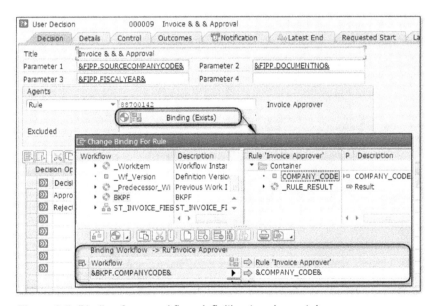

Figure 3.5: Binding from workflow definition to rule container

Figure 3.5 portrays the binding from the workflow definition to the rule container. Container elements can be defined as a class, a BOR object, a DDIC structure, or a DDIC field. They can be defined as single entries or multiline tables. When defining a container element, you can decide if the element will be mandatory or not. In addition, you will notice that the IMPORT/EXPORT settings are greyed out, meaning they can't be changed. The IMPORT parameter is flagged on and the EXPORT parameter is flagged off. This is because container elements only flow into a workflow rule, they are not returned to the workflow.

You may want to capture the selected work item agents in the task container because once the work item is performed, you will only have information on the actual agent. To do this, set binding back to the workflow container. Note, the workflow container will not be populated with the agents. The result will actually end up in the task work item's container. See Figure 3.6 for the binding from the rule.

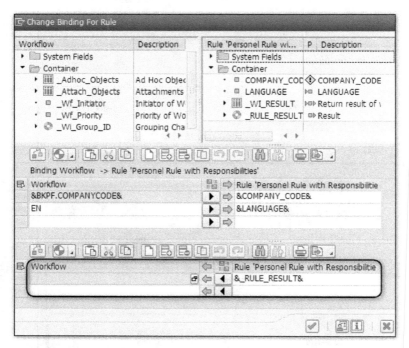

Figure 3.6: Binding from rule back to workflow

The agents returned from the rule will be loaded into a container element with the same name (see Figure 3.7). You can see that it is a single instance of BOR object AAGENT. The BOR object is instantiated with the first agent, but all agents are available in a table named AGENTS that is an attribute of the AAGENT object.

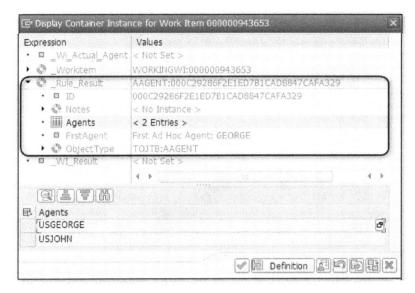

Figure 3.7: Rule result in work item container

3.1 Rules with function modules

A rule that executes a function has the most flexibility because the code is constrained only by using the required function module signature. On the other hand, ABAP code is required which will increase the difficulty of maintenance and support.

See Listing 3.1 for the signature for the function module. It shows the required tables and the one exception that is recognized.

```
FUNCTION Zfunction_module_for_rule.
*"----------------------------------------------------------------
*"*"Local Interface:
*"  TABLES
*"      ACTOR_TAB STRUCTURE  SWHACTOR
*"      AC_CONTAINER STRUCTURE  SWCONT
*"  EXCEPTIONS
```

```
*"        NOBODY_FOUND
*"------------------------------------------------------------
   INCLUDE <cntain>. "Necessary for Container processing Macros
   DATA: ls_actor_tab      TYPE swhactor,
         lv_cont_val_1      TYPE char20,
         lv_cont_val_2      TYPE char20,
         lv_userid          TYPE xubname,
         lt_userid          TYPE TABLE OF xubname.

   REFRESH: actor_tab.
   CLEAR:   lv_cont_val_1, lv_cont_val_2, lv_userid, lt_userid.

*  Get Values from Rule Container
   swc_get_element ac_container CONT1' lv_cont_val_1.
   swc_get_element ac_container 'CONT2' lv_cont_val_2.

   TRY.
*    [include processing logic to obtain users from any table
*    in the system, including a z-table if necessary based on
*    the container values read from the rule container]
     CATCH cx_root.
        RAISE nobody_found.
   ENDTRY.

*  Load Actor_Tab with users found
   IF lt_userid IS INITIAL.
      RAISE nobody_found.
   ELSE.
      LOOP AT lt_userid INTO lv_userid.
        CLEAR ls_actor_tab.
        ls_actor_tab-otype = 'US'.
        ls_actor_tab-objid = lv_userid.
        APPEND ls_actor_tab TO actor_tab.
      ENDLOOP.
   ENDIF.
ENDFUNCTION.
```

Listing 3.1: Function module for rule shell

Agents found may be of the type US for user ID. In addition, your function module may return organizational objects such as organizational units, positions, etc. Figure 3.8 shows how the rule returned a job in this rule simulation. Inside the simulation tool, click on the ⬚ Agent <-> User button to toggle between the organizational object and the users who are resolved from the organizational objects.

If no agents are found from your function module, then you must raise the exception, Nobody Found. The rule will then interpret this exception and, if set to error if no one is found, will issue an error for the workflow (see Figure 3.9).

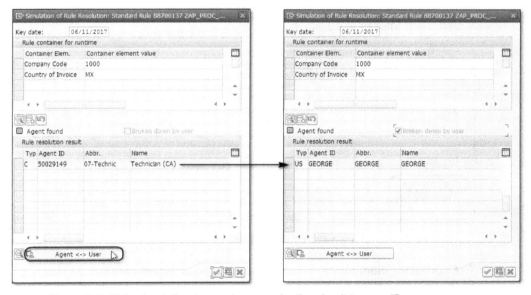

Figure 3.8: Rule simulation to resolve organizational unit to user ID

Rule definition		
Category	Agent Determination: Function to be Executed	▼
Function Module	Z_FUNCTION_MODULE_FOR_RULE	
✓ Terminate If Rule Resolution Without Result		

Figure 3.9: Rule definition if no agent was found

3.2   Rules with responsibilities

Rules with responsibilities allow flexible agent assignment based on real-time object attributes. They are easy for non-technical business users to maintain because no ABAP is required.

To create a rule with responsibilities, as with creating any type of rule, you go to transaction PFAC. You will select the category AGENT DETER-MINATION: RESPONSIBILITIES. When this category is selected, two new checkboxes appear (see Figure 3.10). The check box RESPECT SECOND-ARY PRIORITIES will be discussed later in a workshop, Section 7.1. The other checkbox, PERSONAL RULE, is added as unchecked. This checkbox is discussed later in this section.

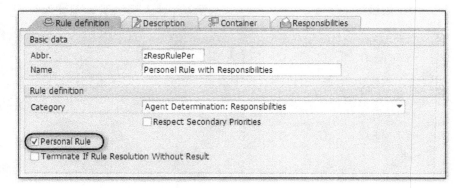

Figure 3.10: Personal rule with responsibilities

The container elements for the rule with responsibilities need to be defined. You may define as many elements as you like, but the fewer you use, the easier the rule will be to maintain. Although it is possible to define container elements for rules with responsibilities as multiline elements, only single fields, single classes, or single BOR objects are supported. Figure 3.11 shows two container elements that have been created; COMPANY_CODE was created as mandatory.

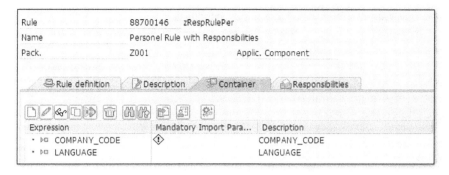

Figure 3.11: Rule container

Once you have created the container elements, you are ready to create the responsibilities. See Figure 3.12 for the definition of a responsibility. Each responsibility will be named, and values will be assigned to container elements.

Multiline container elements

 Multiline container elements for rules with responsibilities are not supported, although you do have the ability to define them as multiline. If you define a container element as something other than a single field, you will not receive an error during rule definition, or even in the workflow definition, but the rule will either not return a result or the list of agents returned will be based on only part of the container element(s) and will not be accurate.

When a responsibility is created, it is assigned a number (see ❶ in Figure 3.12). The EDITING PERIOD, ❷, defaults to the current date through 12/31/9999. This is the validity period for the responsibility. Having validity periods for responsibilities gives you the opportunity to define them to be effective for a future day. In addition, it allows you to delimit responsibilities, as opposed to deleting them. By delimiting instead of deleting, you can retain a history of the responsibilities assigned to the rule. Give an abbreviation and a name to the responsibility ❸. See ❹ for the area where values are assigned to the rule's container elements. Responsibilities give you the flexibility to add single values to the container elements, add a range of values, or add multiple values by single clicking on the name of the container element you want to add another value for and clicking on the INSERT LINE icon 🗒.

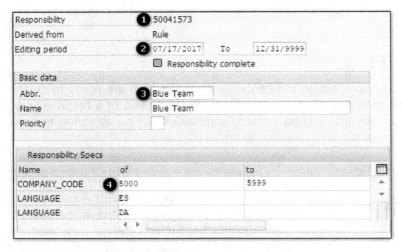

Responsibility	❶ 50041573	
Derived from	Rule	
Editing period	❷ 07/17/2017 To	12/31/9999
	☐ Responsibility complete	
Basic data		
Abbr.	❸ Blue Team	
Name	Blue Team	
Priority		
Responsibility Specs		
Name	of	to
COMPANY_CODE ❹	5000	5999
LANGUAGE	ES	
LANGUAGE	DA	

Figure 3.12: Responsibility definition

As you can see in Figure 3.12, the container element LANGUAGE appears two times with different entries. This is an example of having multiple entries without requiring a range. Unfortunately, there is no way to exclude values as can be done with standard select option functionality.

Responsibility number assignment

The prefix for number ranges on responsibilities is configured as other organizational objects (organizational units, positions, jobs) via transaction OONR, unlike workflow prefixes for number ranges configured using transaction OOW4.

To illustrate how the PERSONAL RULE flag is used, agents have been assigned to responsibilities directly as SAP user ID assignments and indirectly assigned as an organizational unit, which resolves to SAP user ID Donna (see Figure 3.13). When the rule is created, the default value of the PERSONAL RULE field is not flagged. This is the setting to run the first simulation. Looking at ❶ in Figure 3.14, you can see that the organizational object has been included in the simulation. The PERSONAL RULE field was then flagged, and the result of the second simulation is that the organizational object, as shown at ❷ in Figure 3.14, is not included.

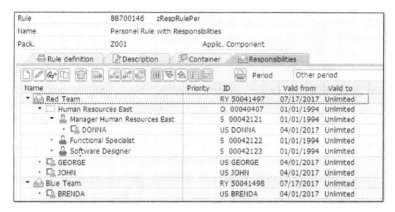

Rule	88700146	zRespRulePer		
Name	Personel Rule with Responsibilities			
Pack.	Z001	Applic. Component		

Name	Priority	ID	Valid from	Valid to
▼ Red Team		RY 50041497	07/17/2017	Unlimited
▼ ☐ Human Resources East		O 00040407	01/01/1994	Unlimited
▼ Manager Human Resources East		S 00042121	01/01/1994	Unlimited
· DONNA		US DONNA	04/01/2017	Unlimited
· Functional Specialist		S 00042122	01/01/1994	Unlimited
· Software Designer		S 00042123	01/01/1994	Unlimited
· GEORGE		US GEORGE	04/01/2017	Unlimited
· JOHN		US JOHN	04/01/2017	Unlimited
▼ Blue Team		RY 50041498	07/17/2017	Unlimited
· BRENDA		US BRENDA	04/01/2017	Unlimited

Figure 3.13: Responsibilities defined as users and org objects

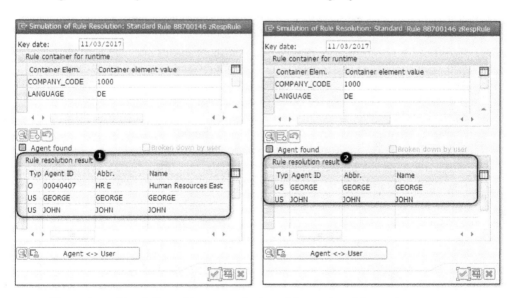

Figure 3.14: Simulation with personal rule not flagged and flagged

The OVERVIEW icon ▦ gives you a way to see the responsibilities and container values at the same time (see Figure 3.15).

Rule: Change

Responsibility	Name	Start date	End Date	COMPA..	COMPA..	LANGUA..	LANGUA..
RY 50041497	Red Team	07/17/2017	12/31/9999	1000	1999	*	
RY 50041499	Green Team	07/17/2017	12/31/9999	3000	3999	E	
RY 50041572	Yellow Team	12/04/2017	12/31/9999	*		*	
RY 50041573	Blue Team	11/11/2017	12/31/9999	5000	5999	K	
RY 50041573	Blue Team	11/11/2017	12/31/9999	5000	5999	S	

Figure 3.15: Responsibility overview

To transport or to recreate...

Rules with responsibilities can have the responsibilities and responsibility relationships transported to production via RHMOVE30, however, most production users are not available in the development environment and it is not possible to transport all the relationships to users and/or personnel IDs. However, it is still nice to have the responsibilities transported. Assigning agents to the responsibilities is all that must happen in each non-development environment. Come up with a strategy for creating responsibilities directly in production via transaction OOCU_RESP or transporting responsibilities and stick with your plan for consistency. As a failsafe, make sure the responsibilities in production have a different number sequence than in development in case there is a mixture of responsibilities transported from the development environment and responsibilities being created directly in production. This will keep the responsibilities from stepping on each other because no responsibility from a development environment will have the same object ID assigned as those assigned in production.

3.3 Rules that read evaluation paths

Rules with evaluation paths allow workflows to take advantage of existing HR relationships and existing HR evaluation paths. HR uses evaluation paths to illustrate the relationships between organizational objects. Evaluation paths can be described as navigation paths, showing the possible relationships of objects and how they interact with other objects, e.g. top-down or bottom-up, or both. Transaction OOAW shows all the evaluation paths delivered by SAP. You can also create your own.

3.3.1 Example rule using an evaluation path

In Section 1.2.2, there is an example using a rule with responsibilities to denote the different languages of AP processors so that invoices in different languages can be routed to the appropriate processors. Someone in HR discovered this and let you know that this information is already maintained in the system and you can access it via an evaluation path.

The information they refer to is in the form of qualifications. Each language supported by the company is represented by its own qualification (see Figure 3.16). Alternatively, each employee may have a language assigned in their personnel record, however, this does not allow assignment of multiple languages to an AP processor, nor does it indicate language aptitude. Transaction PO11 shows the language qualification assignment to the personnel IDs. Figure 3.17 shows the users who are assigned to the Spanish-language qualification. You will use the existing relationship between personnel and qualifications, where the person fulfils the qualification (Relationship: P A32 Q).

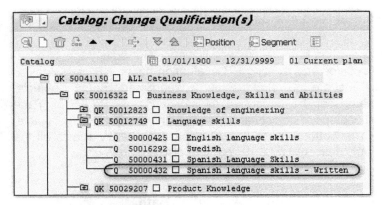

Figure 3.16: Qualifications for languages, t-code OOQA

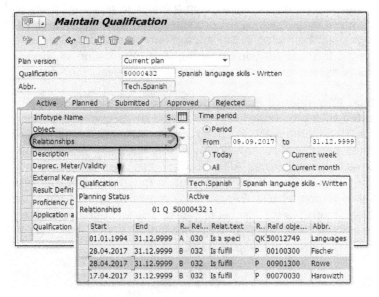

Figure 3.17: Assign qualification to personnel, t-code PO11

You need to pass a qualification to the rule so it can resolve to persons and users with this qualification (see Figure 3.18). Standard evaluation path B032 will take care of the requirements.

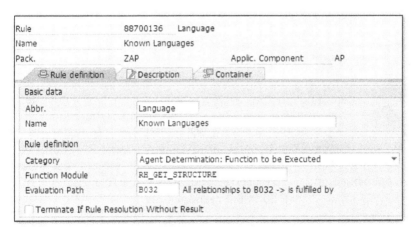

Change View "Evaluation path (individual maintenance)": Overview

New Entries

Dialog Structure	Evaluation Path	B032		Is fulfilled by			
▼ Evaluation paths							
• Evaluation path	No.	Obj. t...	A/B	Reinship	Relationship name	Priority	Rel.obj.type
• Short names	10	*	B	032	Is fulfilled by	*	*

Figure 3.18: Evaluation path B032, t-code OOAW

Now that you know the evaluation path you want to use, you can create the rule. There is no special rule type for evaluation paths. Select the rule type, FUNCTION TO BE EXECUTED and enter the function module, RH_GET_STRUCTURE. The rule definition recognizes this function module and inserts a new field, EVALUATION PATH to collect the evaluation path to be used. As shown in Figure 3.19 the function module is populated, and the EVALUATION PATH selected is B032.

Rule	88700136	Language		
Name	Known Languages			
Pack.	ZAP	Applic. Component	AP	

Rule definition | Description | Container

Basic data

Abbr.	Language
Name	Known Languages

Rule definition

Category	Agent Determination: Function to be Executed ▼
Function Module	RH_GET_STRUCTURE
Evaluation Path	B032 All relationships to B032 -> is fulfilled by

☐ Terminate If Rule Resolution Without Result

Figure 3.19: Rule using evaluation path, t-code PFAC

A rule that reads evaluation paths, using function module RH_GET _STRUCTURE, requires specific container elements to be defined, such as OTYPE type OTYPE and OBJID type ACTORID. See Figure 3.20.

The workflow will pass the required qualification based on the language of the invoice to the rule, and the personnel in the company that possess this qualification will be returned. To correlate the language of the invoice with the proper qualification, create a virtual attribute for business object ZFIPP, which is delegated to FIPP. This attribute will read the qualification using a function module like RHPE_QCAT_BRANCH_READ which will pass the main Qualification QK 50012749 for language skills and have all the language qualifications returned. The virtual attribute will then match up the language on the invoice with the qualification.

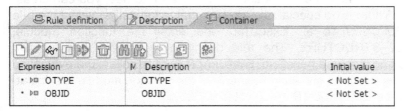

	M	Description	Initial value
☐ Rule definition		☐ Description	☐ Container
Expression		Description	Initial value
• ▷☐ OTYPE		OTYPE	< Not Set >
• ▷☐ OBJID		OBJID	< Not Set >

Figure 3.20: Rule container elements

Rule simulation

Simulating the rule from transaction PFAC will return all personnel in the company who speak this language. Keep in mind, when the rule is called by your workflow, the possible task agents will be used in conjunction with responsibility agents and excluded agents to return the actual agents. When simulating the rule, the agents are not restricted by the possible agents and excluded agents; and the rule results in all the agents who are assigned to the responsibility.

3.4 Rules that read organizational data

SAP allows you to build rules that are based on organizational data. Say there is a new workflow requirement for automating credit approvals. You want to build a rule based on organizational data. Using the BOR browser, transaction swo2, you found the BOR business object T024B, CREDIT MANAGEMENT CREDIT REP. GROUP, and fortunately it already has the appropriate header flag designating this BOR object as ORGANIZATIONAL

TYPE (see Figure 3.21). Additionally, there is a configuration requirement before you can use the BOR object as an organizational object for a rule. Figure 3.22 shows the error message when you insert BOR object T024B as the organizational object type in the rule. The configuration is shown in Figure 3.23.

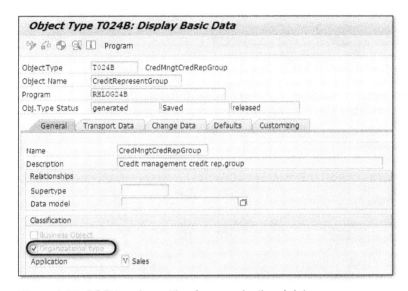

Figure 3.21: BOR header setting for organizational data

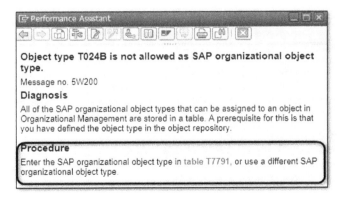

Figure 3.22: Rule error when T7791 configuration is missing

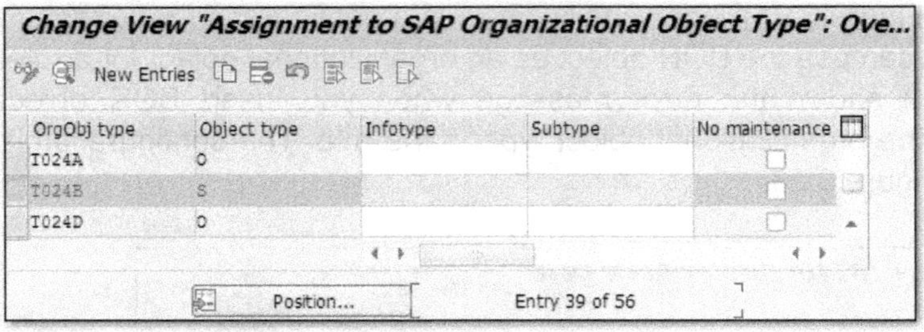

Change View "Assignment to SAP Organizational Object Type": Ove...

New Entries

OrgObj type	Object type	Infotype	Subtype	No maintenance
T024A	O			☐
T024B	S			☐
T024D	O			☐

Position...   Entry 39 of 56

Figure 3.23: Organizational data BOR object configuration T7791

You are ready to build your rule (see Figure 3.24). Note that when you selected the category of the rule as AGENT DETERMINATION: ORGANIZA-TIONAL DATA, the CONTAINER tab is removed. You will not be defining container elements.

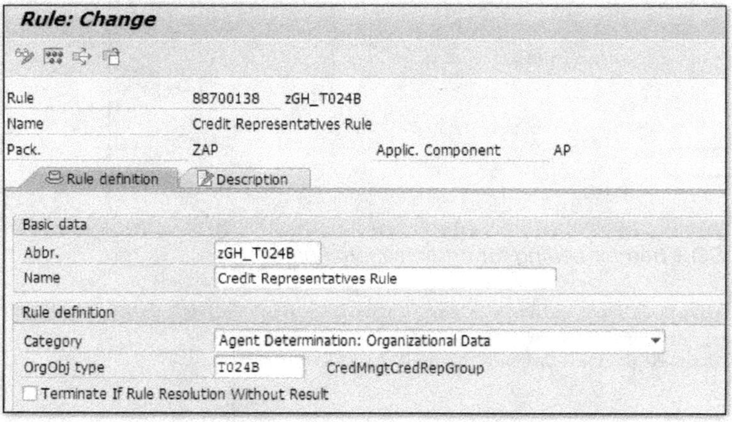

Rule: Change

Rule	88700138	zGH_T024B		
Name	Credit Representatives Rule			
Pack.	ZAP		Applic. Component	AP

Rule definition   Description

Basic data

Abbr.	zGH_T024B
Name	Credit Representatives Rule

Rule definition

Category	Agent Determination: Organizational Data
OrgObj type	T024B CredMngtCredRepGroup

☐ Terminate If Rule Resolution Without Result

Figure 3.24: Rule for organizational object T024B

Now that you supplied the configuration to allow you to assign the credit management organizational data to positions, locate the positions for making the assignment. Transaction PPOM is used to find the positions that will be assigned to this organizational data. Find the positions you want for the assignment in organizational object O 50002662 (see Figure 3.25).

Transaction PFOM is used to build the relationship between the organizational data and organizational units. As shown in Figure 3.26, enter the organization object that contains the positions for the assignments. Also enter the organizational data object **T024B**. Click on the PENCIL button to go to the screen where you select the positions, and click on the ASSIGNMENT icon ⬚. You will be asked to supply the CREDIT REP. GROUP and CREDIT CONTROL AREA. These are the keys to table T024B. Make this same assignment to all three positions listed; single-click the positions as shown in Figure 3.27 at ❶, ❷, and ❸ to select each position and then click on the ASSIGNMENT icon ⬚ to assign the CREDIT REP. GROUP of GLB and the CREDIT CONTROL AREA of 7700.

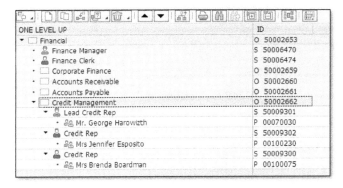

Figure 3.25: Credit management organizational unit

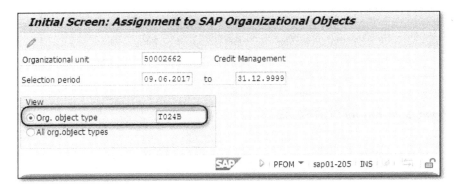

Figure 3.26: Transaction PFOM

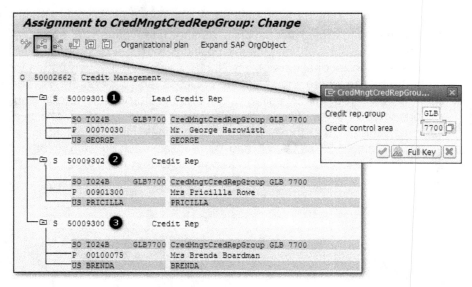

Figure 3.27: PFOM assignment of T024B to positions

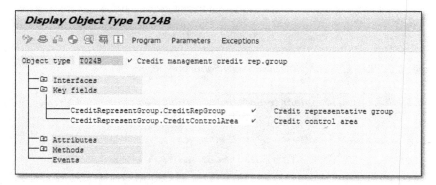

Figure 3.28: Key for BOR T024B

How do you instantiate T024B? Figure 3.28 shows the key fields for business object T024B. The credit approval workflow is based on the sales order. You simply create a virtual attribute of the credit rep group on the sales order object (see Figure 3.29).

Performance tip

 Instead of creating a virtual attribute to instantiate the object, a better way to accomplish this is to create a result method that returns the business object T024B instantiated. If you use a virtual attribute, the code will be processed each time the BOR object is instantiated. By using a result method instead, the code is only processed when it is needed, by calling the method.

Object Type: Editor Edit Program ZBUS2032

```
211     get_property creditrepgroup changing container.
212   TYPES: BEGIN OF ty_crgrp,
213            sbgrp TYPE vbak-sbgrp,
214            kkber TYPE vbak-kkber,
215          END OF ty_crgrp.
216   DATA: ls_crgrp  TYPE ty_crgrp,
217         lv_objkey TYPE swo_typeid.
218   IF object-creditrepgroup IS INITIAL.
219     swc_get_property self 'CreditAgentGroup' ls_crgrp-sbgrp.
220     swc_get_property self 'CreditControlArea' ls_crgrp-kkber.
221     MOVE ls_crgrp TO lv_objkey.
222     swc_create_object object-creditrepgroup 'T024B' lv_objkey.
223     swc_set_element container 'CreditRepGroup' object-creditrepgroup.
224   ENDIF.
225   end_property.
```

Figure 3.29: Sales order virtual attribute for credit rep group

Figure 3.30 shows how the virtual attribute for T024B on the sales order business object populates the rule's mandatory container element ORG_OBJECT_ID.

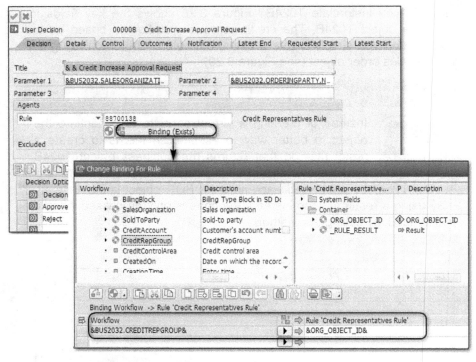

Figure 3.30: Binding to rule for organizational data rule

What BOR objects are set up for organizational data rules?

 Look at table TOJTB where OBJCLASS = '01' to find BOR objects that are set up for organizational data *or* look at table T7791 to see all the BOR objects that are configured for organizational data.

Time to recap. There are three steps that must be completed before you can use the business object by an organizational data rule:

✓ Our BOR object T024B has the appropriate header value of ORGANI-ZATIONAL TYPE checked.

✓ There is configuration in table T7791 for BOR object T024B.

✅ Assignments of organizational objects to SAP organizational data is maintained for via transaction PFOM.

Figure 3.31 shows the agents that are found based on the example above.

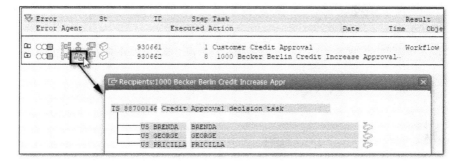

Figure 3.31: Organization data rule agents

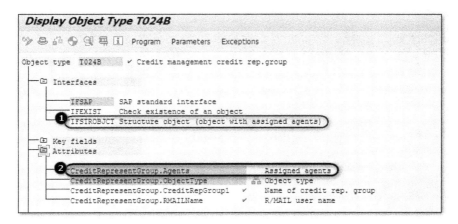

Figure 3.32: Business object T024B with IFSTROBJCT

There is an alternate way to obtain agents for organizational data. Instead of creating an organizational data rule, you can incorporate interface IFSTROBJCT to your BOR object type. See Figure 3.32, ❶. By using this interface, your BOR object will have a new multiline attribute named AGENTS ❷ that will hold the agents assigned.

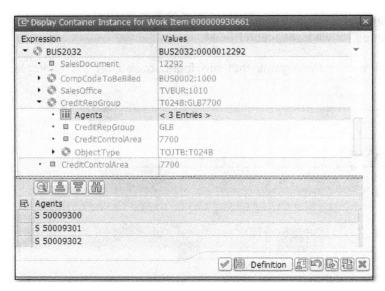

Figure 3.33: Attribute agents of BOR object T024B

Figure 3.33 shows a runtime container instance for the credit workflow. The agents can be seen in a multiline attribute of the BOR object T024B. These are the positions that the rule resolves to SAP user IDs for work item agents. This attribute can be used as an expression to assign agents.

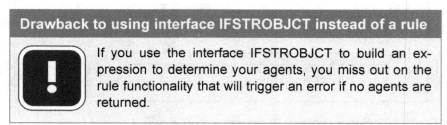

Drawback to using interface IFSTROBJCT instead of a rule

If you use the interface IFSTROBJCT to build an expression to determine your agents, you miss out on the rule functionality that will trigger an error if no agents are returned.

3.5 Rules that read BRF+ decision table

My go-to rule type is a rule with responsibilities. I prefer using this type because it is easy to set up and is so flexible to change after go-live. However, when there are numerous container elements, it can become too cumbersome. In addition, there are many advantages to using a BRF+ decision table over a rule with responsibilities.

Replace your complicated rule with responsibilities with a BRF+ decision table. You can take advantage of the BRF+ rule engine by using a single BRF+ decision table that is accessed by a BRF+ function.

Benefits of BRF+ decision table over responsibilities:

▶ **Versioning.** Although with responsibilities you can delimit responsibilities and responsibility relationships, it is not guaranteed that these will not just be deleted. Versioning can be turned on for BRF+ decision tables and any change can be logged. You can download all versions to MS Excel and you can easily revert to any version you wish.

▶ **Data validation**. You can set up the decision table to only accept valid values for both the container elements and the returning agents. This will ensure accuracy. Even if you decide that valid values are not required, when entering the values, it is nice to see available domain values via a drop-down menu. This functionality is not present with rules with responsibilities.

▶ **Enhanced functionality.**

   ▶ Condition columns (rule container elements) in decision tables have select option capabilities. This means you can include single values or ranges and exclude single values or ranges for each condition column. Using rule with responsibilities, the responsibility values can only include single values or ranges, but cannot exclude single values or ranges.

   ▶ Condition column values in a decision table may contain wild cards anywhere in the character string so that patterns may be included or excluded. Responsibility values can only have a wild card at the end of the character string.

   ▶ Condition column values in a decision table may perform comparisons (greater than or equal to, less than or equal to, etc.).

▶ **User friendliness.** The BRF+ rule engine will display descriptions for all values entered in both the condition and result columns, assuming the elements are mapped to DDIC elements. With responsibilities, you will only see the container element value (e.g. the 4-character plant code instead of the plant code + the plant description).

▶ **Easier maintenance.** You can upload/download the entire decision table from MS Excel. This allows business users to only worry about maintaining a spreadsheet and passing the completed spreadsheet to IT to upload.

▶ **Visibility.** With responsibilities, you can either view the responsibility specifications or you can view the agents assigned to the responsibility. With decision tables, you can pivot and filter both the agents and business object properties used for determining an agent in MS Excel. In addition, with BRF+ decision tables, you control the display order of the rows. This is a huge difference from rules with responsibilities where the responsibilities are in the order of the number assigned when the responsibility is created.

Path for workflow calling a BRF+ decision table

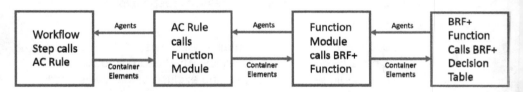

Figure 3.34: Workflow rule to call BRF+ decision table

Figure 3.34 shows the flow of all the objects involved and how they are called, and also how the agents return by each object in the path.

BRF+ function build

Call transaction BRF+ (or transaction BRFPLUS) to build the function and decision table. Create the new BRF+ application first. At the top left corner of the screen click on CREATE APPLICATION (see Figure 3.35).

Figure 3.35: Create BRF+ application

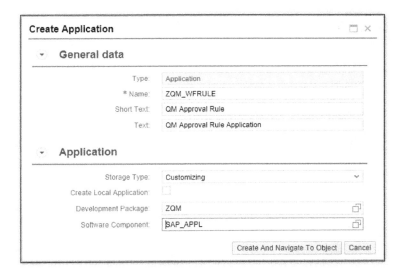

Figure 3.36: Create a BRF+ application

Once you click on CREATE APPLICATION, a new screen appears. See Figure 3.36. You are building a QM approval application and have named it accordingly. Select CUSTOMIZING as the STORAGE TYPE, assign a development package, and list the software component.

Once the application has been created, create the function. From the object tree, right-click on the application name and select CREATE • FUNCTION.

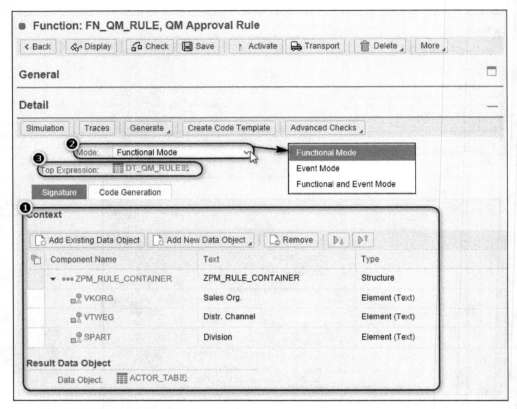

Figure 3.37: Function properties

❶ The signature of the function is made up of the CONTEXT and the RESULT DATA OBJECT. The context is similar to a function module's import parameters and the result data object is similar to the function module's output parameters. You built a structure in SAP's data dictionary named ZPM_RULE_CONTAINER. This structure holds the three fields, as shown in Figure 3.37, that make up the function's context. You created this structure as a data dictionary object in SAP because you will need to create a function module that will call the function. This function module will use this structure as its import parameter.

The RESULT DATA OBJECT in the function's signature will be a table named ACTOR_TAB. This table is defined with the SAP data dictionary table type of TSWHACTOR which is identical to what the rule function modules return.

❷ The function will be defined with mode of FUNCTIONAL, which means that you will define a top expression. If you defined the function as EVENT MODE, then the result would be actions. The top expression is the expression that the function will interact with. The top expression could be any of the following expressions listed in Figure 3.38.

Boolean	Dynamic Expression
Business Rule Management System Connector	Formula
Case	Function Call
Constant	Loop
Create BPEM case	No Action
Create CU	Procedure Call
Create Contact	Random Number
Create Notification EXP	Retrieve BO Data across Related Nodes
Create Service Order	Search Tree
Database Lookup	TRM Method Call
Decision Table	Table Operation
Decision Tree	Value Range

Figure 3.38 BRF+ expression types

❸ The top expression for the function will be a decision table. When you select FUNCTIONAL MODE, the TOP EXPRESSION OF <NOT AS-SIGNED> appears. Click on the CREATE button 📇 and select DECISION TABLE. Because you are creating the decision table from inside the function, the resulting data object, ACTOR_TAB, will be added automatically as the resulting data object of the function. The three fields highlighted in Figure 3.39 must be populated but all other field values default in. Click on CREATE AND NAVIGATE TO OBJECT.

You will see in Figure 3.40 that the decision table header is undefined. Click on TABLE SETTINGS to get to the decision table definition. The condition columns of the decision table correspond to the container elements of the rule and the result column corresponds to the agents returned by the rule (see Figure 3.41).

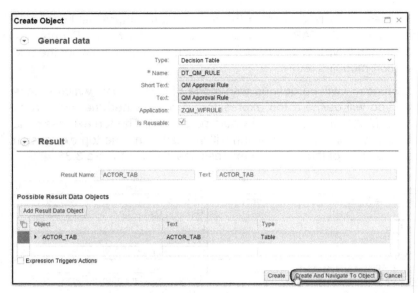

Figure 3.39: Decision table creation

Figure 3.40: Empty decision table

Have the decision table mimic the rule result

Set up the result columns of the decision table to correspond to the export table of your function module, which will be the result of your rule. This is a table of structure TSWHACTOR (OTYPE + OBJID).

Figure 3.41: Decision table, table settings

❶ RETURN ALL MATCHES FOUND means that you expect a table to be returned. This could only be one record, but it will be returned as a table instead of a structure. This is selected so that multiple agents can be returned. If this is not checked, then the first record found will be returned as a structure. Keep in mind, the order matters. Rows will be read from the top to the bottom and the first match will be returned.

❷ SPLIT RESULT DATA OBJECT INTO COLUMNS check box, if checked, will break the result columns into individual columns as displayed in Figure 3.41 ❻. This allows the attributes, MANDATORY INPUT and COLUMN ACCESSIBILITY to be applied differently to each column. If it is not checked, then the result columns will show as a table. The attributes are then assigned to the entire row instead of at the column level.

❸ The resulting data object is defaulted in from the function.

73

❹ and ❺ are settings that have the following options:

▶ Show messages as errors

▶ Show messages as warning

▶ Do not show any messages

▶ Application default

Stick with the application default, which is defined at the application level in the DETAIL section, DEFAULTS SETTINGS (see Figure 3.50).

❻ RESULT COLUMNS are defaulted in from the function.

❼ CONDITION COLUMNS need to be included. You will add them from the context data objects. This context comes from the calling function.

Figure 3.42: Inserting condition columns

When the context objects are shown, you see structure ZPM_RULE_CONTAINER, as shown in Figure 3.37. Select all three fields and click OK to have them populate in the decision table condition columns, see Figure 3.43. Check sales organization (VKORG) and distribution channel (VTWEG) as MANDATORY INPUT.

Once you click on the OK button you will be returned to your empty decision table. You can click on the INSERT ROW 🖹 button to add a new row (see Figure 3.44).

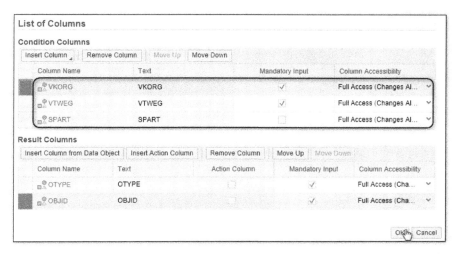

Figure 3.43: Condition and result columns of decision table

Figure 3.44: Add a row to decision table

Alternatively, you can take advantage of how easy it is to populate an Excel spreadsheet to load your data (see Figure 3.45).

Figure 3.45: Export empty decision table to Excel

As shown in Figure 3.46, a template is built for you to enter your decision table condition column data and result column data. Note the different column heading colors. Condition columns are given a darker shade than result columns. This distinction is important because the types of values that can be entered are different. Help for what can be entered in these columns is found in the downloaded template. See Figure 3.49.

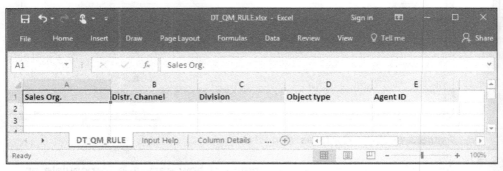

Figure 3.46: Blank Excel template

Excel template tip

The robust functionality of a decision table can be confusing for Excel entry. If you require logic in your condition columns, it might be a good idea for you to build one row of data from inside the BRF+ rule engine and then download this one row of data with your Excel template so you have an example of how BRF+ wants to receive your data.

The Excel template also includes information on how the columns are defined in the BRF+ decision table. See Figure 3.47.

	A	B	C	D	E	F	G	H	I	J	K
		Description	Result					Only	Only Upper	Time point	Dimen-
1	Name	(Text)	Column	Type	Binding	Length	Decimals	Positive	case	Type	sion Key
2	VKORG	Sales Org.		Element (Text)	VKORG	4	0		X		
3	VTWEG	Distr. Channel		Element (Text)	VTWEG	2	0		X		
4	SPART	Division		Element (Text)	SPART	2	0		X		
5	OTYPE	Object type	X	Element (Text)	OTYPE	2	0		X		
6	OBJID	Agent ID	X	Element (Text)	ACTORID	12	0		X		
7											
8											

◄ ► ... | Input Help | Column Details | Column Alias Ma ... ⊕ | ◄ |

Figure 3.47 Decision table column details

Once your spreadsheet is complete, you will upload and activate it. You can then run a quick unit test by simulating the decision table. BRF+ allows you to simulate at the expression level. Expressions are decision tables, decision trees, formulas, etc.

Sales Org.	Distr. Channel	Division	Object type	Agent ID
1000	10	00	US	LORI
1000	12	09	US	GARY

Figure 3.48: BRF+ decision table example entries

	A	B	C
3	Condition columns take range expression as their cell values		
4	Range Option	Pattern	Example
5	contains any	contains any &1	contains any abc
6	contains only	contains only &1	contains only abc
7	contains string	contains string &1	contains string abc
8	currency equals	currency equals	currency equals EUR
9	does not contain any	contains not any &1	contains not any abc
10	does not contain only	contains not only &1	contains not only abc
11	does not contain string	contains no string &1	contains no string abc
12	does not match pattern	[<>&pattern]	[<>pattern]
13	ends with	ends with &1	ends with abc
14	is between	[&1..&2]	[0..15]
15	is equal to	=&1	=abc
16	is greater than	> &1	> 100
17	is greater than or equal to	>= &1	>=200
18	is initial	is initial	is initial
19	is less than	< &1	<100
20	is less than or equal to	<= &1	<=200
21	is not between	<&1;>&2	<12;>50
22	is not equal to	<>&1	<>abc
23	is not initial	is not initial	is not initial
24	is not valid	is not valid	is not valid
25	is valid	is valid	is valid
26	matches pattern	[&pattern]	[pattern]
27	starts with text	starts with &1	starts with abc
28	unit equals	unit equals	unit equals KG
29			
30	Result columns take constant expression as their cell values		
31			
32	Range Option	Pattern	Example
33	or	&1 ; &2	EUR ; USD
34	(and) unless	exclude &1	exclude JPY
35			
36	Result Column Type	Pattern	Example
37	Text	&1	abc
38	Number	NUMBER	123 , 200.50
39	Boolean	TRUE/FALSE (change the cell format	TRUE , FALSE
40	Amount	NUMBER CURRENCY	100 USD
41	Quantity	NUMBER UNIT	100 KG
42	Timepoint - Date Format	YYYY-MM-DD	2011-01-06
43	Timepoint - Date Time Format	YYYY-MM-DDThh:mm:ss	2011-01-06T10:10:10
44	Timepoint - Timestamp Format	YYYY-MM-DDThh:mm:ssZ	2011-01-06T10:10:10Z
45	Timepoint - Time Format	Thh:mm:ss	T10:10:10
46	Timepoint - Date Time with offset Form	YYYY-MM-DDThh:mm:ss[+|-]hh:mm	2011-01-06T10:10:10+10:00

| DT_QM_RULE | Input Help | Column Details ... |

Figure 3.49: Excel BRF+ decision table input help

Decision table priorities options

 If you want multiple records returned from your decision table, one thing you will lose if using one decision table instead of a rule with responsibilities is the ability to have priorities. You can still use priorities using a single BRF+ decision table, but you will need to incorporate a ruleset.

Set up your BRF+ function to call a BRF+ ruleset. This ruleset will in turn contain multiple rules that can be prioritized. Each rule of the ruleset can read your BRF+ decision table in a different way (e.g. the first rule will read the decision table with all container elements, the second rule will read the decision table with fewer container elements, until an agent is returned).

If you only want one record to be returned, you can have prioritization with only the decision table based on the order of the rows. Place the rows you want to give a higher priority at the top, and lower priorities at the bottom. The first row that is read that fits will be the one returned.

Versioning

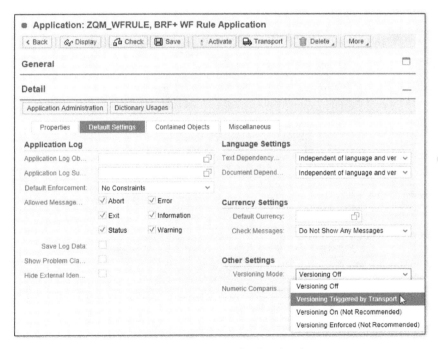

Figure 3.50: Turn versioning on at the application level

BRF+ provides excellent versioning. You can set the versioning to create a version for every change, or to only create a version based on a transport. If changes are made to the BRF+ object directly in a production environment (e.g. the BRF+: exit is used and method if_fdt_application_settings~get_changeability has been coded to allow changes), it is a good idea to turn versioning on. Figure 3.51 shows how different versions can be compared. You can easily revert back to any previous version.

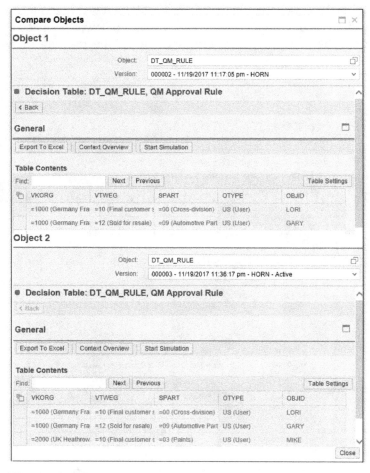

Figure 3.51: Compare object versions

Build a rule that uses the BRF+ application

Once the BRF+ application has been created, you can build a rule that will call it. Figure 3.52 depicts the model of an SAP Workflow rule calling a BRF+ function. The circled part is the rule calling the function module which calls the BRF+ function module. The function module will be built with the standard interface the workflow rule expects. The signature of the BRF+ function is built to return a table of agents, exactly the way the workflow rule will return the agents.

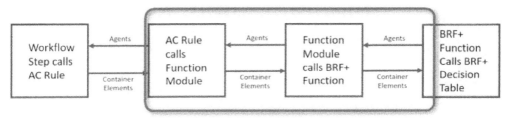

Figure 3.52: Rule and function module to call BRF+ function

First, build the function module that will call the BRF+ function. From inside the BRF+ function, go to GENERATE • FUNCTION MODULE (RFC), see Figure 3.53.

Figure 3.53: Generate function module from BRF+ function

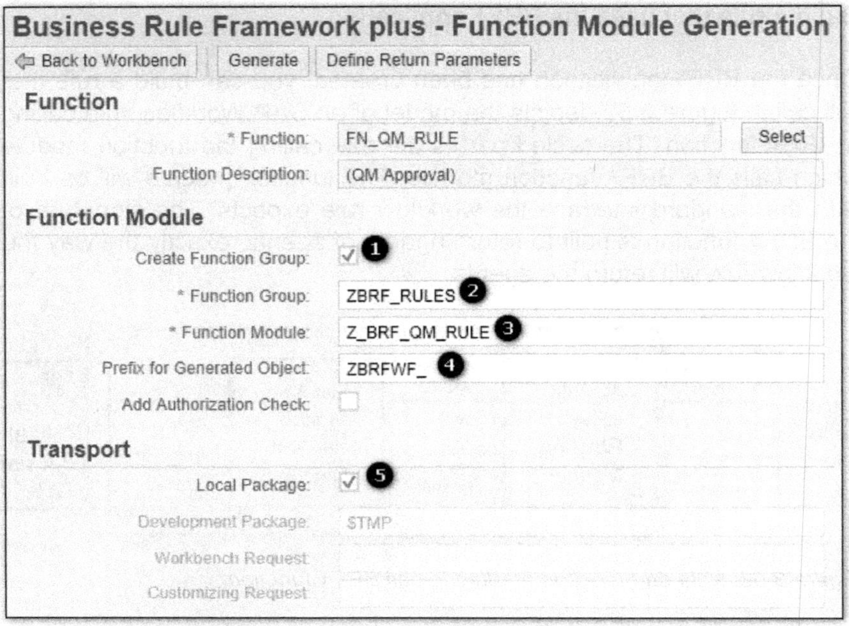

Figure 3.54: Function module generation

Referring to Figure 3.54, to build the function module, you need to give direction for what will be built in the backend system. In the example, you are creating a new function group, so click on the ❶ CREATE FUNCTION GROUP checkbox. ❷ is where you name the function group. ❸ is where you name the function module. The function module generator creates new data dictionary structures and table types for the function module interface. These new DDIC objects are named using a GUID. The generator allows you to give a prefix for these names. Define the prefix for the DDIC options at ❹. Finally, ❺ is where you define the package and transport information. You are creating a local package for this example.

The generated code is shown in Listing 3.2. The generated import and export parameters are shown in Figure 3.55.

```
FUNCTION Z_BRF_QM_RULE.
  DATA _vr_data TYPE REF TO data.
  DATA _vr_data_ext TYPE REF TO data.
  DATA _vs_name_value_pair TYPE abap_parmbind.
```

```
      DATA _vts_name_value_pair TYPE abap_parmbind_tab.
      DATA _v_timestamp TYPE if_fdt_types=>timestamp.
      FIELD-SYMBOLS <_v_any> TYPE any.
      FIELD-SYMBOLS <_v_any_tab> TYPE any table.

*  Get current timestamp for processing
      GET TIME STAMP FIELD _v_timestamp.

*  Prepare context for function processing
         CLEAR _vr_data.
         CLEAR _vs_name_value_pair.
      GET REFERENCE OF ZPM_RULE_CONTAINER INTO _vr_data_ext.
      cl_fdt_function_process=>move_data_to_data_object(
         EXPORTING
            ir_data          = _vr_data_ext
            iv_function_id   = '000C29286F2E1ED790FBB51FA415A30E'
            iv_data_object   = '000C29286F2E1ED790FC788E4209430E'
            iv_timestamp     = _v_timestamp
            iv_trace_generation = ''
         IMPORTING
            er_data          = _vs_name_value_pair-value ).
         _vs_name_value_pair-name = 'ZPM_RULE_CONTAINER'.
      INSERT _vs_name_value_pair INTO TABLE _vts_name_value_pair.

   TRY.
      CLEAR _vr_data.
      GET REFERENCE OF E_ACTOR_TAB INTO _vr_data.
*****************************************************************
* Trigger function processing
*****************************************************************
      ASSIGN _vr_data->* TO <_v_any>.
      CALL METHOD cl_fdt_function_process=>process
         EXPORTING
            iv_function_id = '000C29286F2E1ED790FBB51FA415A30E'
            iv_timestamp = _v_timestamp
         IMPORTING
            ea_result = <_v_any>
         CHANGING
            ct_name_value = _vts_name_value_pair.
      E_ACTOR_TAB = <_v_any>.
```

```
CATCH CX_FDT_NO_RESULT.
  MESSAGE ID 'SFDT_CODE_COMPOSER' TYPE 'E' NUMBER '039'
  RAISING CX_FDT_NO_RESULT.
CATCH CX_FDT_ARITHMETIC_ERROR.
  MESSAGE ID 'SFDT_CODE_COMPOSER' TYPE 'E' NUMBER '040'
  RAISING CX_FDT_ARITHMETIC_ERROR.
CATCH CX_FDT_PROCESSING.
  MESSAGE ID 'SFDT_CODE_COMPOSER' TYPE 'E' NUMBER '041'
  RAISING CX_FDT_PROCESSING.
CATCH CX_FDT.
  MESSAGE ID 'SFDT_CODE_COMPOSER' TYPE 'E' NUMBER '041'
  RAISING CX_FDT.ENDTRY.
ENDFUNCTION.
```

Listing 3.2: Generated function module code

Figure 3.55: Function module import and export parameters

Now create a function module that has the signature required for a work-flow rule like Listing 3.3. The function module will simply call the BRF+ generated function module.

Combine function modules

Combine the BRF+ generated function module into the function module that can be called by a workflow rule. See Section 7.2.3 for an example.

```
FUNCTION z_wf_rule_qm.
*"------------------------------------------------------------
*"*"Local Interface:
*"  TABLES
*"      ACTOR_TAB STRUCTURE  SWHACTOR
*"      AC_CONTAINER STRUCTURE  SWCONT
*"  EXCEPTIONS
*"      NOBODY_FOUND
*"------------------------------------------------------------
  INCLUDE <cntain>.
* data elements defined with structure created by BRF+
* function module generator.
  DATA: ls_rule_cont TYPE zbrfwf_003n7kf14ic8c1rweq71mon,
        lt_brf_actor TYPE zbrfwf_003n7kf14ic8c1sgzzzxul3,
        ls_brf_actor TYPE zbrfwf_003n7kf14ic8c1sgzzzy0wn.
  swc_get_element ac_container 'VKORG' ls_rule_cont-vkorg.
  swc_get_element ac_container 'VTWEG' ls_rule_cont-vtweg.
  swc_get_element ac_container 'SPART' ls_rule_cont-spart.

  CALL FUNCTION 'Z_BRF_QM_RULE'
    EXPORTING
      zpm_rule_container     = ls_rule_cont
    IMPORTING
      e_actor_tab            = lt_brf_actor
    EXCEPTIONS
      cx_fdt                 = 1
      cx_fdt_no_result       = 2
      cx_fdt_arithmetic_error = 3
      cx_fdt_processing      = 4
      OTHERS                 = 5.
  IF sy-subrc = 0.
```

```
    APPEND LINES OF lt_brf_actor TO actor_tab.
  ELSE.
    RAISE nobody_found.
  ENDIF.
ENDFUNCTION.
```

Listing 3.3: Rule function module to call BRF function module

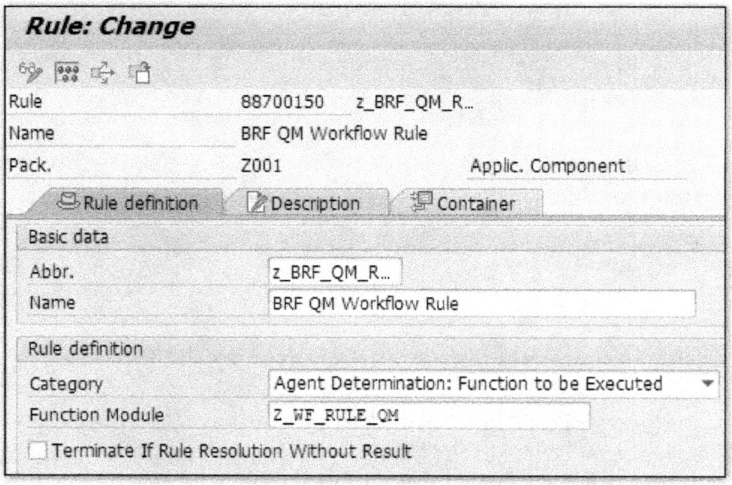

Figure 3.56: Workflow function module rule definition

Lastly, create a rule that calls your rule function module. See Figure 3.56. Once you have created your rule, you can run a quick simulation. See Figure 3.57. The simulation of the rule is based on the data in the decision table, as shown in Figure 3.48.

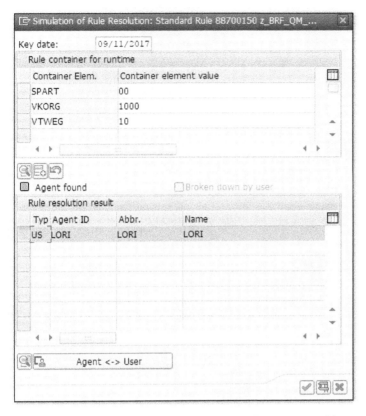

Figure 3.57: Simulation of rule that reads BRF+ decision table

4 SAP Business Workplace

It is critical to understand the functionality available to agents for processing work items, so you can support them as their workflow administrator. This chapter focuses on SAP Business Workplace functionality that pertains to agents.

You can get to the SAP Business Workplace by clicking on the INBOX icon 📝 from the SAP EASY ACCESS menu or by calling transaction SBWP.

4.1 Agent-centric functionality

4.1.1 Forwarding work items

The task attributes determine if a work item can be forwarded inside or outside of the possible agents or not at all.

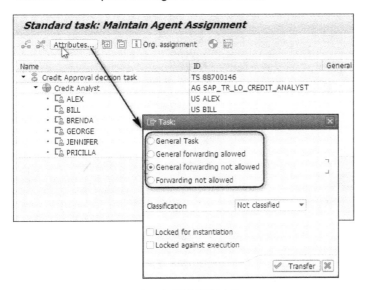

Figure 4.1: Attributes of task TS88700146

▶ *General forwarding allowed* means that the work item can be forwarded to users who are not possible agents.

▶ *General forwarding not allowed* means that the work item can be forwarded to users who are possible agents.

▶ *Forwarding not allowed* means that the work item cannot be forwarded to anyone.

▶ *General task* means that there is no indication of forwarding abilities associated with a task set as a general task, but if a task is set as a general task, the work item may be forwarded to any user.

The example task in Figure 4.1 has the setting that general forwarding is not allowed. This means that a work item of this task can only be forwarded to the possible agents listed on the task. Figure 4.3 shows the possible agents of an example work item of task TS88700146, with the selected agents indicated.

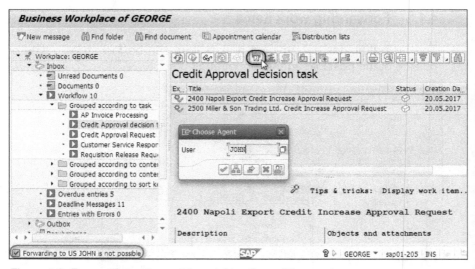

Figure 4.2: Forwarding not possible outside of possible agents

See Figure 4.2 for the error message George receives when he tries to forward a work item outside the pool of its possible agents. Following the unsuccessful attempt to forward the work item, George successfully forwarded the work item to Bill, who is in the work item's pool of possible agents. Figure 4.4 shows how the work item is now only in Bill's inbox.

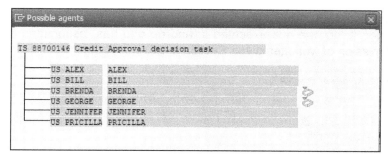

Figure 4.3: Possible agents of work item

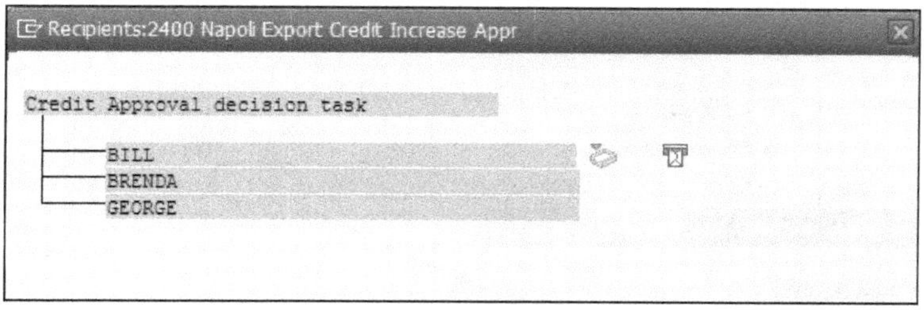

Figure 4.4: Recipients after work item was forwarded

Note: If general forwarding is allowed for a task, the person forwarding the work item will be able to forward the work item to users who are not possible users, however, they will receive the following pop-up (see Figure 4.5).

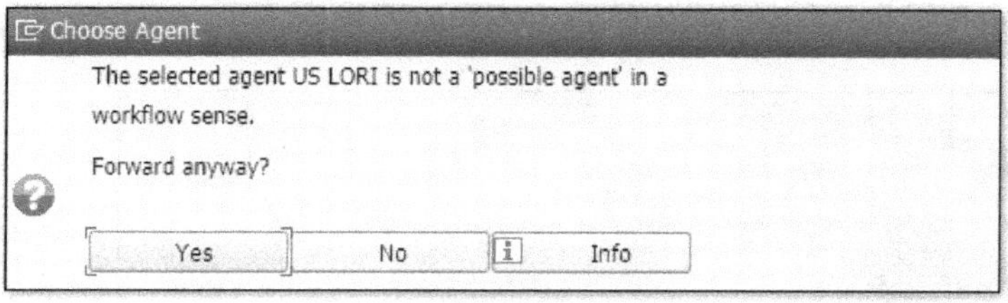

Figure 4.5: General forwarding warning pop-up

4.1.2   Reserve and replace work items

Reserve and replace functionality is used by work queues. A work queue is established when more than one agent receives the same work item in their inbox. For example, all the agents in Figure 4.6 can see the work item for invoice 1000 1900000007 2017 because no one in the queue has reserved it, no one has executed it, and no one has resubmitted it (for resubmission of work items see Section 4.1.3).

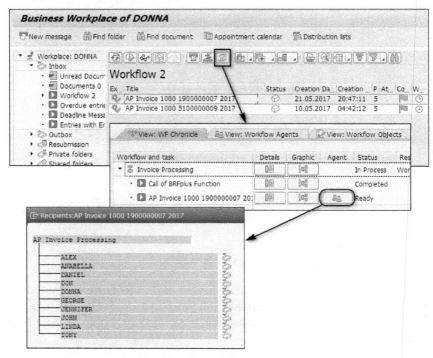

Figure 4.6: Queue of agents available for processing AP invoices

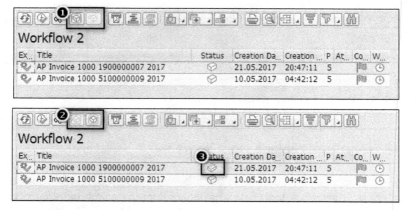

Figure 4.7: Reserve and replace toggle icons

If someone in the queue executes a work item from the queue or re-serves a work item from the queue, it will have the same effect: the work item will be removed from all the inboxes of the users in the queue. This functionality is necessary so that multiple people will not waste time working on the same work item. If a user, after executing a work item, decides they do not want to work on it at that time, they simple need to place it back into the queue so others can again see the work item in their inboxes.

Refer to Figure 4.7 for an example of SAP Business Workplace reserve and replace functionality.

❶ User Donna has selected invoice 1900000007. The RESERVE icon can be clicked because the invoice is not yet reserved.

❷ Once she clicks on the RESERVE icon, the REPLACE icon immediately toggles on and the user now can place the work item back into the queue.

❸ While the work item is reserved, the WORK ITEM STATUS Icon will have a flag on it.

Figure 4.8 is the inbox of another agent in the queue. Now that Donna has reserved invoice 1000 1900000007 2017, it is no longer visible in Tony's inbox.

Figure 4.8: Tony's workplace with missing invoice

If a user executes a work item, but then is not able to complete the pro-cessing, the work item will also be removed from the queue. If the user decides that they no longer want to be responsible for processing the work item, they will cancel out of processing the work item and click on the REPLACE icon to place it back into the queue. While the work item is reserved, it is not visible to other users who are also agents of the task.

4.1.3 Resubmission of work items

A user may decide they want to process a work item at a later date. If they want this work item out of their inbox until the later date, they can resubmit the work item by clicking on the RESUBMIT ![icon] icon. The user will be prompted to enter a resubmission date.

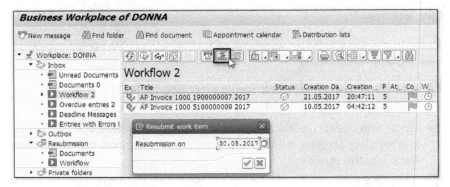

Figure 4.9: Resubmission of work item

Once the resubmission date has been entered, the work item will be removed from the inbox and placed in the resubmission folder. Note the WAITING STATUS ![icon] icon, Figure 4.10, ❶. The work item remains in the resubmission folder until the date selected at midnight, system time.

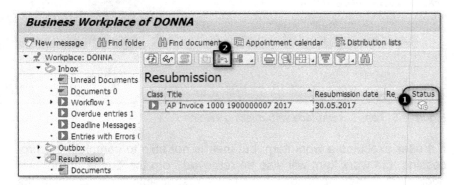

Figure 4.10: Resubmission folder

It is possible to execute the work item from the resubmission folder if the user decides they want to process the work item before the resubmission date. In addition, the user can click on the END RESUBMISSION icon ![icon], as shown in Figure 4.10, ❷, and the work item will immediately return to the user's workflow inbox.

Resubmission in a work queue

If a work item has multiple agents and is placed in resubmission status by one of the agents, it is automatically reserved by that agent. Figure 4.9 shows Donna's work item inbox before she resubmits invoice 1000 1900000007 2017. You can see that the invoice is not reserved by Donna because the WORK ITEM STATUS icon is not the status with a flag 🏴. You can see in Figure 4.11 that the work item is now in resubmission by the waiting status. Clicking on the recipients, you can see that the work item is only in Donna's inbox.

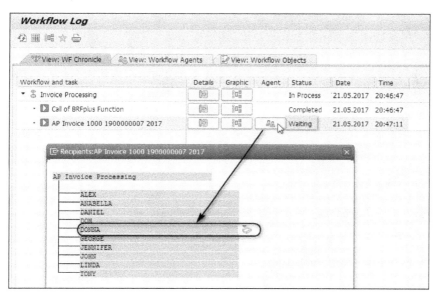

Figure 4.11: Resubmitted work item automatically reserved also

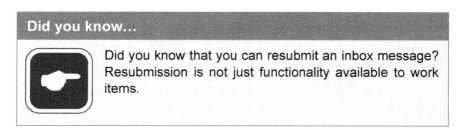

Did you know...

Did you know that you can resubmit an inbox message? Resubmission is not just functionality available to work items.

Donna then clicks on the END RESUBMISSION icon 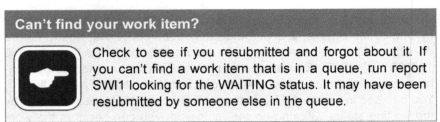 and the work item is returned to her main inbox in reserved status, as shown in Figure 4.12. If she wants the work item to return to the queue, she must replace the work item into the queue.

Can't find your work item?

Check to see if you resubmitted and forgot about it. If you can't find a work item that is in a queue, run report SWI1 looking for the WAITING status. It may have been resubmitted by someone else in the queue.

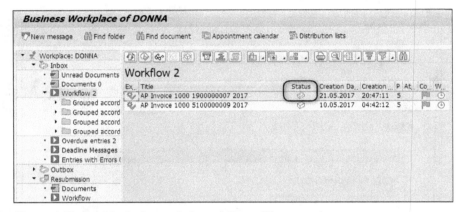

Figure 4.12: Resubmission ended, work item still reserved

4.1.4 Reject processing

A common development question is…should the workflow send an email, or should it send a work item that executes the display of some business object? There are pros and cons to each. The reason an email often wins out, even though the display transaction provides much more information, is because users don't want to be forced to execute a work item if they don't need to display the business object to get additional information. The reason they would have to execute the work item is to complete it and have it removed from their inbox. Rejecting the processing allows the user to clear their SAP Business Workplace without having to view unwanted business objects. Processing can be rejected from the SAP Business Workplace (see Figure 4.13).

Reject processing is only possible if the developer changes the PROCESSING CAN BE REJECTED setting on the DETAILS tab of the workflow step (see Figure 4.14). Note: This setting is part of the workflow definition on the workflow step and not inside the task.

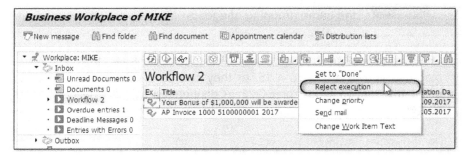

Figure 4.13: Reject processing

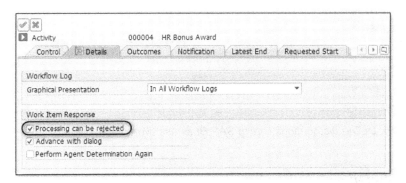

Figure 4.14: Workflow definition requirement to reject execution

4.2 Distribution lists

A distribution list is a collection of people, organizational objects, and/or email addresses that can be notified of an event that occurs in SAP, sent reminders of work to be performed, or even perform a task, if populated with SAP user ID. Distribution lists can be read by the workflow to obtain agents in a similar way that the workflow could use organizational objects (organizational units, jobs, positions, or work centers) to find agents.

Check existing distribution lists first

Before you decide to build a work center or some other organizational object to build a list of agents, make sure there is not already an existing distribution list that holds the same grouping of agents.

Distribution lists are defined and maintained in the SAP Business Workplace as shown in Figure 4.15, or they can be created and maintained using transaction SO15 or SO23. A distribution list can be defined as shared or private.

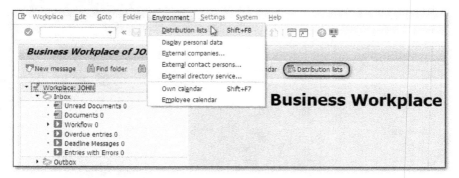

Figure 4.15: Define distributions lists in SAP Business Workplace

4.2.1 Shared distribution list

You have defined a distribution list for financial auditors, as shown in Figure 4.16. This distribution list is not intended to be subscribed to by users, it will be maintained centrally. However, users with sufficient authorization may also edit it. In this distribution list, you have included SAP user IDs, an organizational unit (position), and an email address (see Figure 4.17).

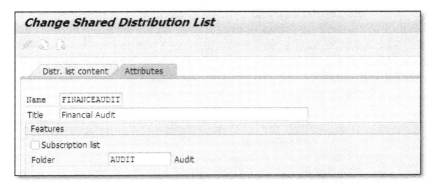

Figure 4.16: Shared distribution list definition

Figure 4.17 shows the recipients on a distribution list:

❶ The default recipient type is an SAP user ID. When SAP user IDs are added to a distribution list, the type is not shown.

❷ Send as express checkbox—this will send a dialog box to inform the user that an express document has been sent, allowing him/her to switch to the inbox.

❸ Send as copy checkbox—the user receives the document as a copy and does not need to take any action.

❹ Send as blind copy checkbox—recipient is a blind recipient.

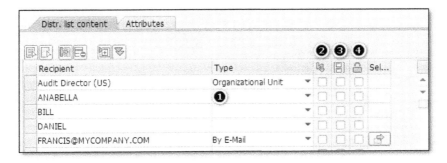

Figure 4.17: Shared distribution list definition—recipients

Distribution lists can be used to find workflow agents. SAP delivers rule AC 30000012 which performs agent determination for a distribution list. See Figure 4.19. No container elements except the distribution list name are required for the rule. There is no functionality available to obtain a subset of the users on the distribution list based on workflow runtime data, as with the functionality available using responsibilities.

You can see from the simulation in Figure 4.18 that the rule can only use SAP user IDs and organizational objects that resolve to SAP user IDs. The one organizational unit entered, position 50003807, will resolve to SAP user ID John when you click on the TOGGLE button ⎣⎕ Agent <-> User⎤. The email address on the distribution list is not usable by the workflow through this rule, so it is not displayed.

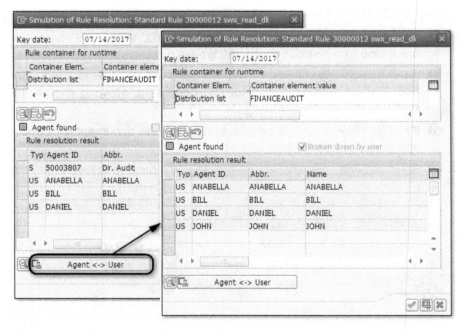

Figure 4.18: Simulation of distribution list rule

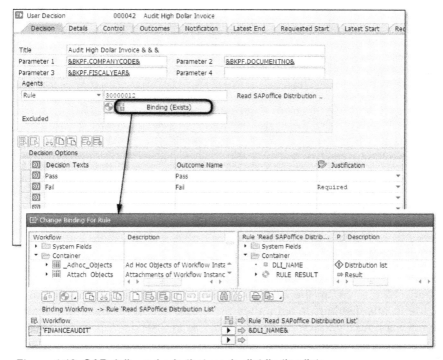

Figure 4.19: SAP delivered rule that reads distribution lists

4.2.2 Shared distribution list with subscription

One benefit to using a distribution list over an organizational object is that users can subscribe to a distribution list, whereas organizational objects must be maintained centrally by someone in HR. Although user training for how to subscribe to a distribution list will be required, the distribution list maintenance is pushed to the user.

SAP allows users to subscribe to business objects, such as a purchase order via GOS (see Figure 4.20). Subscribers will be notified of all changes to the business object. But what if a user wants to be notified of *new* business objects, such as a new vendor? There is no vendor record existing to subscribe to. You can, however, create a simple single-step task that will take subscribers to the vendor display transaction to show them the new record.

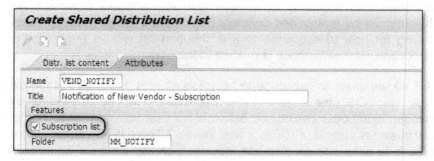

📄 ⬛	**Standard PO 414-0100 Created by GRAUENHORST**				

Do	Create... ▶	⬛ ⬛ Print Preview	Messages [i] ⬛ Personal Setting	
	Attachment list			
⬛ H	Private Note	⬜ Vendor	1000 C.E.B. BERLIN	Doc. dat
⬛	Send ▶			
⬛ E	Relationships	Short Text	PO Quantity	O... C Net Price Curr.
	Workflow ▶	Diaminobenzene 50%	1,500 KG W	2.47 DEM
	My Objects ▶	Add to My Objects	1,500 KG W	3.05 DEM
	Help for object services	Subscribe/cancel object ⬚	1,400 KG W ⬚	1.21 DEM
40	500-150	Natriumhydrogencarbona...	1,400 KG W	2.04 DEM
50	500-160	CAT_01 Catalyst 01 50.	1,200 KG W	1.28 DEM
60	500-170	Diamino Toluene 50%	1,200 KG W	1.51 DEM

Figure 4.20: Subscribing to a purchase order via GOS

Example: Notify users of newly created vendor

Create a new shared distribution list that uses a subscription list. See Figure 4.21. Click on the SUBSCRIPTION LIST check box. Users will subscribe to this distribution list if they are interested in receiving a notification of each new vendor. An example of this is SAP user Daniel subscribing to the distribution list. Daniel will go to his SAP Business Workplace and click on ⬚ Distribution lists or he will use the path: ENVIRONMENT • DISTRIBUTION LISTS. See Figure 4.15. Daniel will search for the new distribution list, VEND_NOTIFY (see Figure 4.22). Daniel will double-click on the distribution list and be taken to the screen where he can subscribe. Daniel can toggle between subscribing and canceling his subscription (see Figure 4.23).

Create Shared Distribution List	
⬚ ⬚ ⬚	
Distr. list content / Attributes	
Name	VEND_NOTIFY
Title	Notification of New Vendor - Subscription
Features	
✓ Subscription list	
Folder	MM_NOTIFY

Figure 4.21: Creation of subscription list

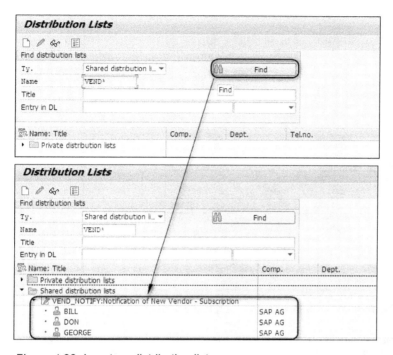

Figure 4.22: Locate a distribution list

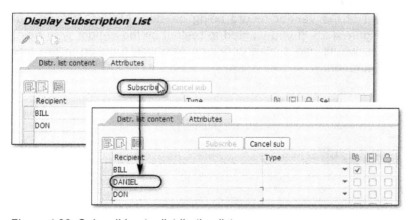

Figure 4.23: Subscribing to distribution list

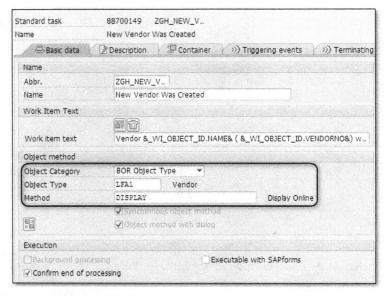

Figure 4.24: Task to notify distribution list recipients of new vendor

Now create a single-step task with the default rule, AC 30000012, provided by SAP that will read your distribution list. The BOR object for the
vendor is LFA1 and the method for displaying the vendor master data,
DISPLAY, is called, as shown in Figure 4.24. The task will have the triggering event of the vendor record being created, LFA1-CREATED, as
shown in Figure 4.25. If you wanted to restrict by the vendor type being
created, you would use a start condition or check function in the type
event configuration.

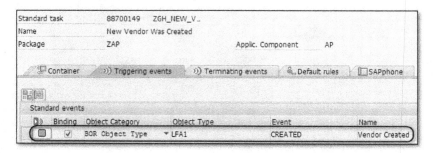

Figure 4.25: Triggering event for displaying a new vendor task

For binding to the default rule, send the distribution list name, VEND_NOTIFY as a constant value, see Figure 4.26. The possible agents for this task will contain multiple roles that allow vendor master data to be displayed.

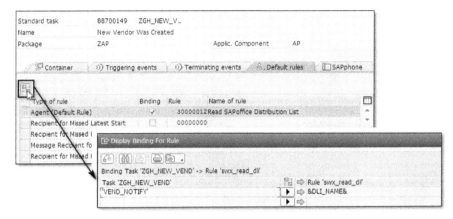

Figure 4.26: Binding for default rule

When a new vendor is created and the workflow runs, the workflow instance log shows that the users from the distribution list are agents of the workflow step (see Figure 4.27).

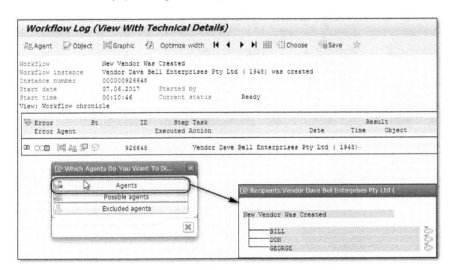

Figure 4.27: Agents of a single-step task are distribution list members

4.3 Adopting views

From SAP Business Workplace, you may adopt other inbox views using evaluation paths (transaction OOAW). A view allows you to view someone else's work items.

View configuration

To configure a view, run transaction SWLV, or use the SAP Customizing Implementation Guide, SAP NETWEAVER • APPLICATION SERVER • BUSINESS MANAGEMENT • SAP BUSINESS WORKFLOW • BASIC SETTINGS • SET UP VIEWS FOR BUSINESS WORKPLACE. See Figure 4.29 for an example configuration.

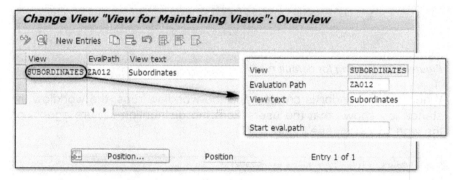

Figure 4.28: Configure a view, transaction SWLV

The view will point to an evaluation path.

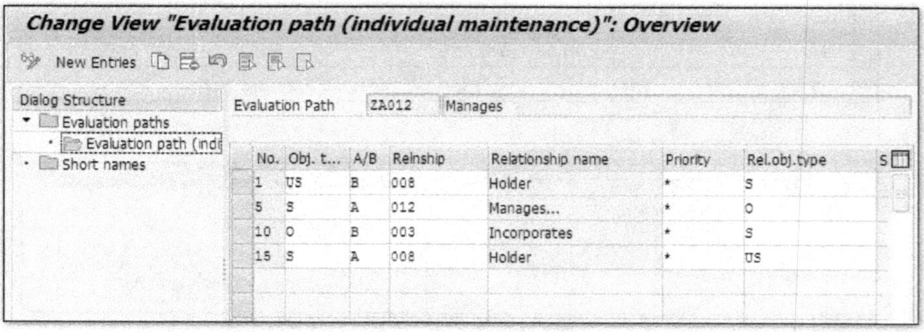

Figure 4.29: Configure evaluation path, transaction OOAW

To illustrate how the view works, look at the business workplaces of George and his two subordinates, Brenda and Pricilla.

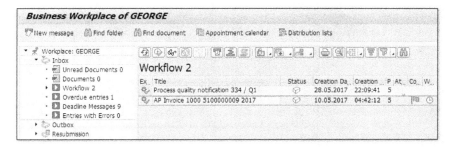

Figure 4.30: George's business workplace

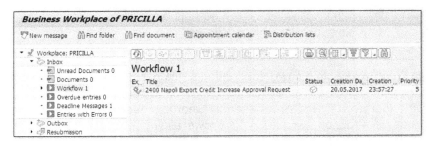

Figure 4.31: Brenda's business workplace

You can see in Figure 4.30, Figure 4.31, and Figure 4.32 that all three users have different work items in their business workplaces. Figure 4.33 shows George first selecting the SUBORDINATES view and then from there he will select his two subordinates, Brenda and Pricilla. All users can see and select the SUBORDINATES view, but only those with actual subordinates will have users to select.

Business Workplace of PRICILLA

New message   Find folder   Find document   Appointment calendar   Distribution lists

- Workplace: PRICILLA
  - Inbox
    - Unread Documents 0
    - Documents 0
    - Workflow 1
    - Overdue entries 0
    - Deadline Messages 1
    - Entries with Errors 0
  - Outbox
  - Resubmission

Workflow 1

Ex.	Title	Status	Creation Da...	Creation	Priority
	2400 Napoli Export Credit Increase Approval Request		20.05.2017	23:57:27	5

Figure 4.32: Pricilla's business workplace

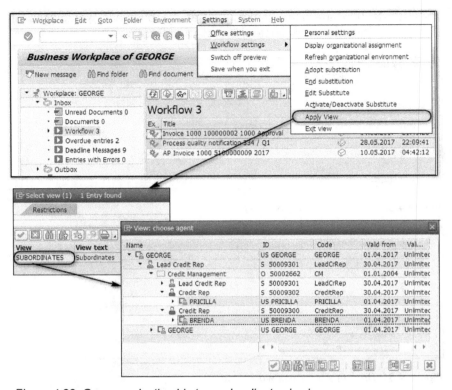

Figure 4.33: George selecting his two subordinates in view

 Evaluation path tip

Build the evaluation path in a way that the user can select themselves, in addition to other users, for the view.
As shown in Figure 4.33, George can select his own
name, allowing him to see his work items in addition to
his subordinate's work items.

Once George selects his two subordinates, his business workplace view
changes. Please see Figure 4.34 to see which folders are George's and
which folders are Brenda's as seen in George's business workplace at
the time of adoption. Figure 4.35 shows all the work items from the
workflow folder belonging to Brenda.

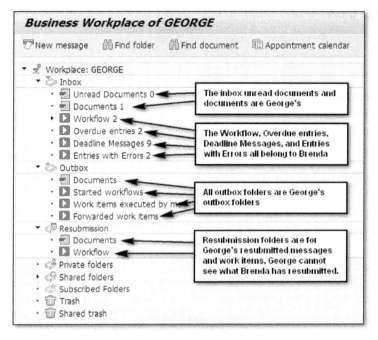

Figure 4.34: George with adopted view of Brenda's

Resubmission fact

If George has adopted Brenda's view, he can resubmit any of her open work items. If he resubmits one of Brenda's work items, it will show up in his resubmission folder, not Brenda's.

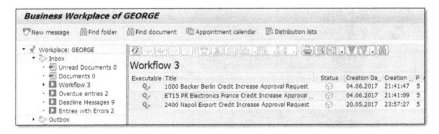

Figure 4.35: Business workplace of George with view active

To deactivate the view and return to your own business workplace go to SETTINGS • WORKFLOW SETTINGS • EXIT VIEW, see Figure 4.36.

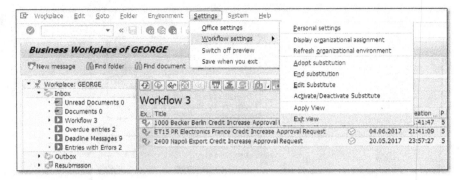

Figure 4.36: Exit view

If you log out while SAP Business Workplace has a view applied, the next time you log in and click on your inbox's WORKFLOW folder, a pop-up will ask if you would like to continue with this view. Figure 4.37 shows George logging in after he previously logged out with Brenda's view active. George clicks on his WORKFLOW folder in his inbox, then receives a pop-up message that shows all the previously active views.

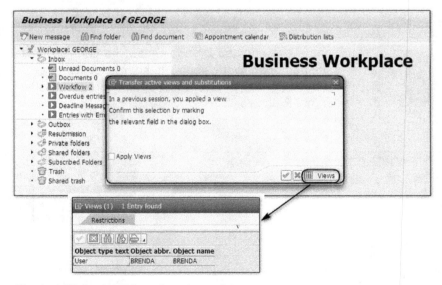

Figure 4.37: Login while active view exists

Privacy concern

If some work items are sensitive or private, you may decide to use *substitution with classification* (see Section 4.5). *Adopting views* does not allow you to be selective regarding which work items are available in the view and which are not. *Substitution with classification* will allow you to select at the task level which work items can be seen by your substitute and which cannot.

4.4 Substitution

Agents take vacation, get sick, have babies, or take time off from work for any number of reasons. When work item agents are absent, it is very helpful if they set up substitutes to perform their work while they are gone. It is not imperative if the agent is part of an agent group that processes work items collectively. However, if the absent agent is often the only work item agent, then to ensure work is processed in a timely manner, a substitute should be specified.

Active vs. passive substitution

There are two ways a substitute can be defined, either as an *active substitute* or as a *passive substitute*. Active substitution is set up by either the agent who will be absent from work or an administrator. It requires no setup action by the substitute. Passive substitution differs from active in that it is initiated by the agent who will be absent, but must subsequently be accepted, or adopted, by the substitute.

To set up active substitution, start in the business workplace of the agent who is going to be absent, and go to SETTINGS • WORKFLOW SETTINGS • EDIT SUBSTITUTE (see Figure 4.38). In this example, Linda is setting Mike to be her substitute. Once Linda selects EDIT SUBSTITUTE, a pop-up appears. She will single-click on her name to select it and then click on the ASSIGNMENT icon . She will be given a pop-up to select the user she wants to be her substitute. She selects Mike and then receives a pop-up asking for VALIDITY (a date range), PROFILE, and whether the substitution

111

is to be active or not (see Figure 4.39). Linda selects the date range for her two-week vacation; she does not choose a substitution profile (substitution profiles will be discussed in Section 4.5). Linda wants to make the substitution active, so she clicks on the SUBSTITUTION ACTIVE checkbox.

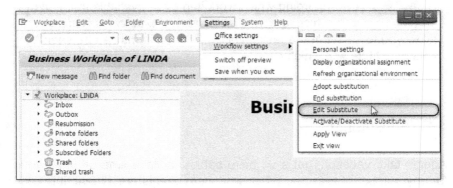

Figure 4.38: Active substitution, step 1

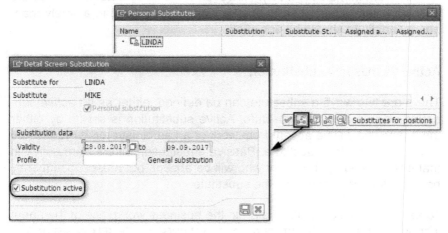

Figure 4.39: Active substitution, step 2

Linda can deactivate the substitution at any time by going to SETTINGS • WORKFLOW SETTINGS • ACTIVATE/DEACTIVATE SUBSTITUTE (see Figure 4.28). It might be easier for the agent to have a substitution set up that will not expire. The agent can then toggle from activate to deactivate as needed, see Figure 4.40.

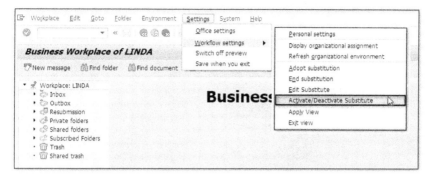

Figure 4.40: Substitution activation/deactivation toggle

To set up passive substitution, the agent would follow the same steps as creating an active substitution, but would leave the SUBSTITUTION ACTIVE checkbox empty. The substitution is not in effect until the substitute adopts the substitution.

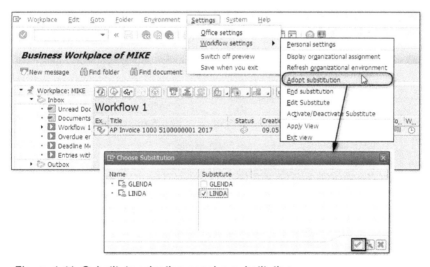

Figure 4.41: Substitute adopting passive substitution

As shown in Figure 4.41, Mike is adopting the substitution of Linda's workplace. Figure 4.42 shows Mike's workflow inbox now that passive adoption of Linda's workplace has happened. Notice that Mike can no longer see his work item, AP INVOICE 1000 5100000001 2017. When a passive adoption of a substitution is made, then the substitute can only see the workplace and work items for which they are the substitute.

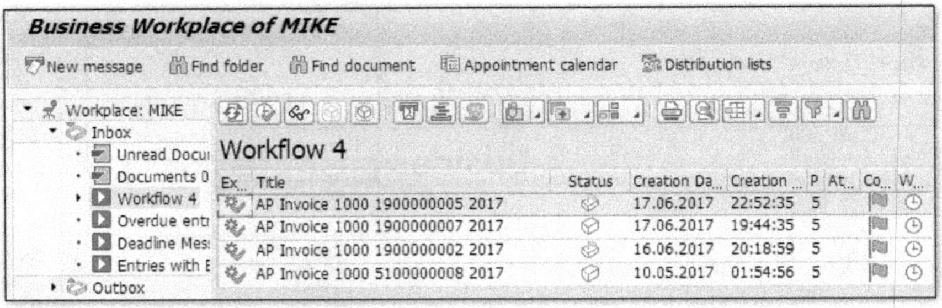

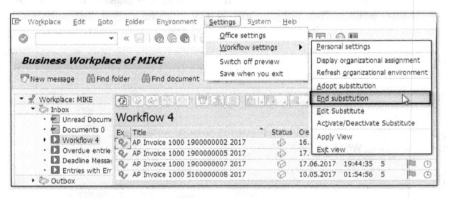

Figure 4.42: Workplace after substitution adopted

To end the passive substitution, the substitute clicks on END SUBSTITUTION from the menu (see Figure 4.43).

Figure 4.43: End passive substitution

If a substitute does not end the substitution manually, the next time they go into SAP Business Workplace they will be asked if they want to continue the substitution (see Figure 4.44).

When the substitute receives this pop-up, they have the choice to view all the agents for whom they previously adopted substitution. They can choose to apply them all again by clicking the APPLY SUBSTITUTIONS checkbox or they can just click the GREEN CHECKMARK button and be taken to their own workplace.

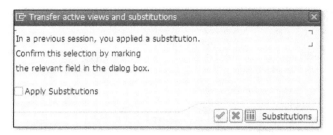

Figure 4.44: Pop-up to continue substitution

Passive substitution vs. active substitution

The SAP Business Workplace inbox view differs greatly for active substitution and for passive substitution. Active substitutes can see their workplace work items and the workplace work items for whom they are a substitute at the same time. On the other hand, passive substitutes must make a choice of which workplace work items they can see. They can view either their own workplace work items or the adopted workplaces of the agents they are substituting for. Note that the passive substitute can choose to adopt multiple workplaces or one at a time for any agent who has set them up as a passive substitute.

Personal or HR positional substitution

All the examples shown so far have been personal substitutions, which is the substitution of a user for the agent as a user. You can also make substitutions based on HR positions. A user, from inside their business workplace, can assign a user, personnel ID, or an HR position to any position they hold.

To assign a positional substitute, you begin in the same way a personal substitute is created (see Figure 4.45). Clicking on EDIT SUBSTITUTE will take you to the screen depicted in Figure 4.46. Lori sees her user ID and she can make substitute assignments to it as personal substitutes, or she can toggle to SUBSTITUTES FOR POSITIONS and be taken to a screen similar to what is shown in Figure 4.47. Lori sees the position she is assigned to and under that she sees her personnel record.

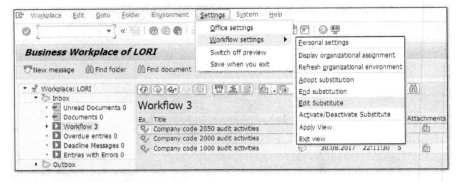

Figure 4.45: HR positional substitution

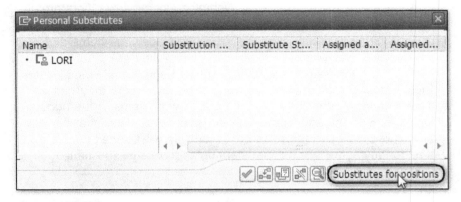

Figure 4.46: Toggle to SUBSTITUTES FOR POSITIONS

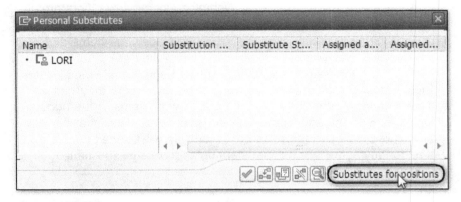

Figure 4.47: Toggle back to PERSONAL SUBSTITUTES

To make an assignment, Lori will single-click her position and then click on the ASSIGNMENT icon 🖻 and will be asked to assign a user ID, personnel ID, or a position. Lori wants to set up her boss, the AUDIT DIRECTOR, to be her substitute whenever she is away. She has the end date set to UNLIMITED and can activate and deactivate the substitution as needed (see Figure 4.48). Notice that the AUDITOR position is at the top, and both Lori and her boss, Mike, are below the position. This is because the assignment is made to Lori's position and not to Lori. If Lori is moved out of the position, then whoever takes over this position will have this substitution assignment already.

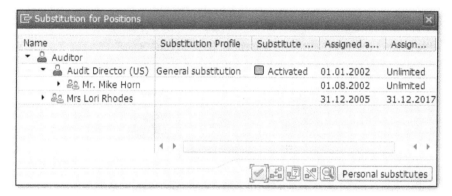

Figure 4.48: Positional substitution

Substitution facts

▶ Even while substitution is active, the original agent has access to and can process all their work items, that is, the work items that have not been reserved or resubmitted by someone else.

▶ A substitute does not need to be a possible agent of the work item task, regardless of forwarding restrictions of the work item.

▶ A substitute will not see work items if they are an excluded agent.

▶ Substitutes are not listed as agents of the task.

▶ A substitute can see work items from the original agent's inbox and their resubmission folder.

▶ A substitute can see work items that are reserved by the original agent of the work item; they show up as reserved in the substitute's inbox.

▶ A substitute can resubmit a work item that belongs to the original agent and the work item is no longer visible to the original agent.

▶ If a substitute reserves a work item that belongs to the original agent, once the substitution period has ended or is deactivated, the work item will still be reserved by the substitute.

The substitute can see why they received a work item when they are not listed as an agent. One way to see this is from the work item display, GOTO • AGENT • SUBSTITUTING FOR… (see Figure 4.49). Mike can see that he received this work item because he is substituting for Lori.

Figure 4.49: Substituting for…

4.5 Substitution classification

It may be necessary to classify work items as work-related vs. personal. This is important when substitution is used. If someone goes on vacation, they will want their substitute(s) to take care of their invoice approvals, but certainly would not want their substitute(s) seeing their HR work items which may contain personal information. This has been made clear with the example shown in Figure 4.49, where Lori has Mike as a substitute and he received her HR notification.

Classification works by defining classifications for tasks and classification profiles for users. The task classifications are assigned to tasks and the classification profiles are assigned to SAP user IDs, SAP personnel IDs, or HR positions. A task can only be assigned to one classification. A single SAP user ID, SAP personnel ID, or an HR position that is defined as a substitute may only have one substitution profile assigned. You may define each substitute with a different substitution profile or no substitution profile at all. It may seem limiting to say that each substitute can only substitute for a single classification, however, multiple task classifications can be assigned to a substitution profile, so you can create all the substitution profiles containing all the task classification combinations you may need.

Substitution classification works the same way for both personal substitution and HR positional substitution. The examples included in this section are of personal substitutions in an effort to make it easier to explain.

SAP Business Workplace comes standard with four task classifications: PROFESSIONAL, PERSONAL, DISCIPLINARY, and NOT CLASSIFIED (see ❶ in Figure 4.50). These should be sufficient, but a new task classification, APPROVAL is added to illustrate how it is done. This classification can be used to distinguish approval work items from other work items. SAP Business Workplace also delivers standard substitution profiles that contain task classifications (see ❷ in Figure 4.50). The 0004 APPROVAL substitution profile was added so there is a profile to correspond with the

APPROVAL task classification. In the IMG task, ASSIGN SUBSTITUTE PRO-FILE, there were two entries created (highlighted and shown in Figure 4.50 by ❸). Substitution profile 0004 now is associated with tasks that have the classification of NO_CLASS, meaning they are not classified, and it is associated with the new APPROVAL classification. By adding NO_CLASS to the profile, the substitute will have all the unclassified work items and the approval tasks. This eliminates having to go back and classifying all the existing tasks that were never classified.

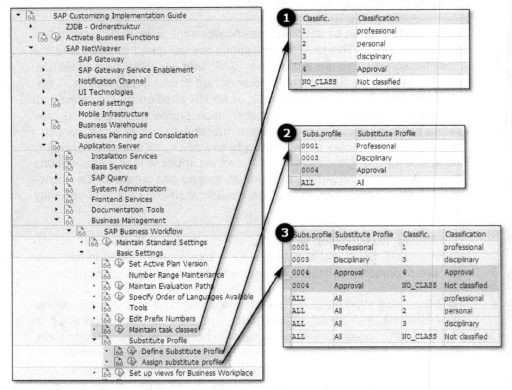

Figure 4.50: Classification and substitution profile configuration

To use the classification functionality, go to your task definition of an HR task. Figure 4.51 shows how to get to the area of the task to make this assignment.

Figure 4.52 shows the classification assignment PERSONAL to this human resources task. Note that this classification screen is another place to assign your task as a general task. Human resource tasks are often set as general tasks because HR tasks pertain to people outside the business functions they perform.

In the next example, Bill is going to go on vacation and he wants Donna to process any new vendor work items he may receive in his absence. Bill wants Anabella to process any of his AP invoice approvals and requisition release work items. Bill goes to his business workplace and sets Donna to be an active substitute for work items that fall into the PROFESSIONAL profile. This means that only work items that are classified as professional can be processed by Donna as a substitute, see Figure 4.53.

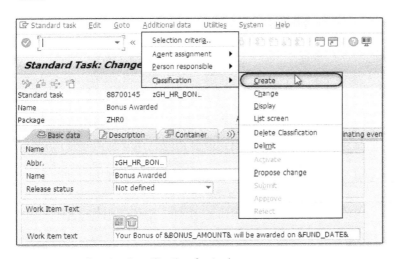

Figure 4.51: Create classification for task

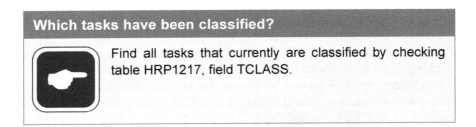

Which tasks have been classified?

Find all tasks that currently are classified by checking table HRP1217, field TCLASS.

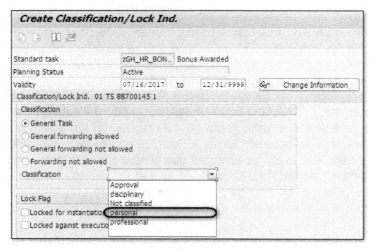

Figure 4.52: Assignment of task classification to task

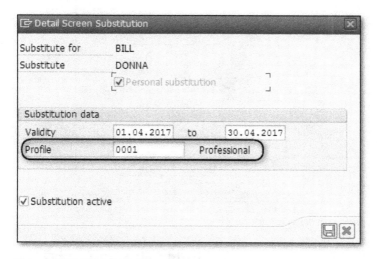

Figure 4.53: Set up of personal active substitute

Different people or positions can be set up to be substitutes for different profiles. Bill set Anabella up to be his substitute for the new APPROVAL substitution profile. Figure 4.54 shows the two substitutes Bill has chosen and each corresponding substitution profile. Note, when Bill created the substitutes, he activated them.

Figure 4.55 shows all the work items for which Bill is an agent. This includes an AP invoice processing work item, a requisition release request, a new vendor notification, and an HR work item regarding a bonus he will be awarded.

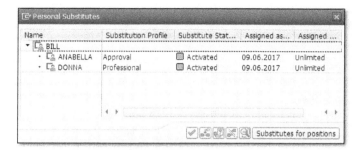

Figure 4.54: Bill's substitutes

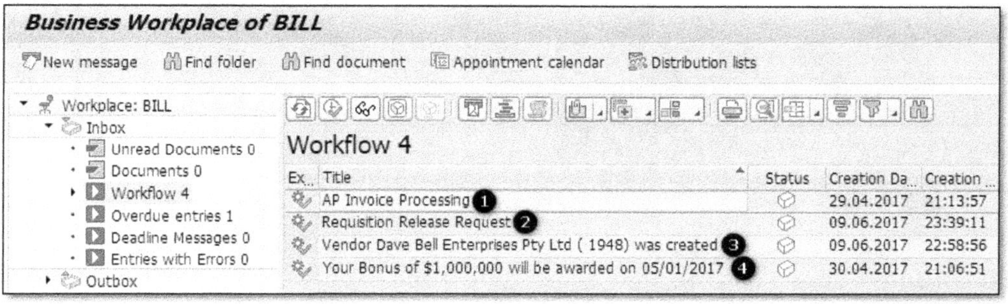

Business Workplace of BILL

Figure 4.55: BILL'S BUSINESS WORKPLACE

Each work item in Bill's inbox has a different task classification, see Figure 4.55.

❶ AP INVOICE PROCESSING—Task classification: None

❷ REQUISITION RELEASE REQUEST—Task classification: APPROVAL

❸ Vendor Dave Bell created—Task classification: PROFESSIONAL

❹ Bonus work item—Task classification: PERSONAL

Donna is a substitute for Bill for work items with the task classification of PROFESSIONAL (see Figure 4.54).

Donna's business workplace entries are shown in Figure 4.56:

▶ Donna does not have Bill's AP invoice processing work item in her workplace because this work item is not classified. As shown in Figure 4.50, the only task classification that is part of the PRO-FESSIONAL substitution profile is the task classification with the same name.

▶ Donna does not have the requisition release work item because this work item has the task classification of APPROVAL. She does not have the bonus work item because this work item has the task classification of PERSONAL. Donna's substitute profile of PROFESSIONAL does not include these task classifications.

▶ The new vendor work item is Bill's only task that has the classification of PROFESSIONAL and that is why it is visible in Donna's business workplace.

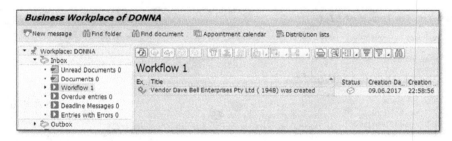

Figure 4.56: Donna's business workplace

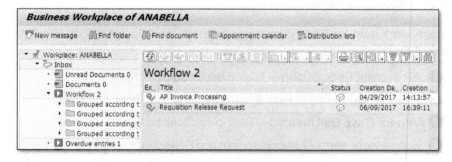

Figure 4.57: Anabella's business workplace

Anabella is a substitute for Bill for work items with the task classification of APPROVAL (see Figure 4.54).

Anabella's business workplace entries (Figure 4.57):

▶ The AP invoice processing task *is* visible in Anabella's inbox because this task is not classified and the classification profile for Approval includes tasks that are not classified.

▶ Anabella does not have the new vendor work item because this task has the task classification of Professional. She does not have the bonus work item because this work item has the task classification of Personal and Anabella's substitute profile of Approval does not include these task classifications.

▶ Anabella does have the requisition release work item in her business workplace because this work item is classified as Approval.

Keep it simple

 The delivered classification Professional will most likely take care of your needs. However, you may want to tweak the configuration to make it easier to use if your company does not currently take advantage of classifying tasks. When tasks are created, they are not classified by default. If you begin to classify tasks and assign classification profiles to users or positions, the substitutes will now only receive the work items that are classified. If you would like them to also receive the ones that are not classified, then add a line of configuration to the Assign Substitute Profiles IMG customizing task (see Figure 4.50). If you want to use the classification profile Professional, then simply add a new entry that assigns the task classification NO_CLASS to profile 0001 Professional.

Subs.profile	Substitute Profile	Classific.	Classification
0001	Professional	1	professional
0001	Professional	NO_CLASS	Not classified

This way, you can find the tasks that should be classified as Personal and keep these work items out of the inboxes of substitutes; and not have to worry about going back to classify all the tasks as Professional.

5 Agent reporting

There are many workflow reports that focus on the agents of work-flow instances. These reports are good for showing errors, pinpointing areas that can be improved, and revealing bottlenecks in the workflow processes.

5.1 Workload analysis

To access the workload analysis report, go to SAP MENU • BUSINESS WORKFLOW • DEVELOPMENT • REPORTING • WORKLOAD ANALYSIS or use transaction SWI5.

This report is used to report on tasks that are completed and tasks waiting to be completed. In Figure 5.1, you can see how the report defaults to COMPLETED WORK ITEMS as the analysis type. The alternative analysis type is WORK ITEMS TO BE COMPLETED.

5.1.1 Completed work items

Figure 5.1 shows the report being run for a single task. The section named, SELECT RESPONSIBILITY is left blank. This means that everyone who has completed an instance of this task as of May 01, 2017 will be reported. Figure 5.2 shows the report results.

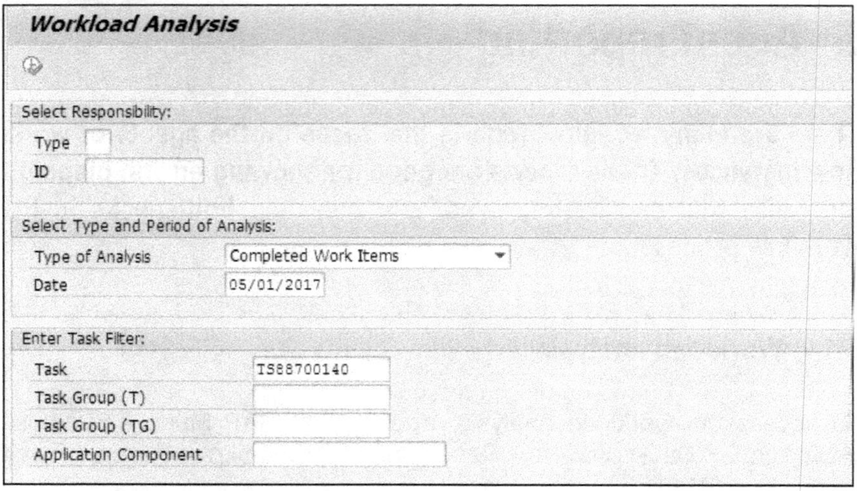

Figure 5.1: Completed work items for a task selection screen

Figure 5.2: Completed work items for a task

Alternatively, this report can be run for a single user. Figure 5.3 shows all the completed work items for one user, Alex, since April 14, 2017.

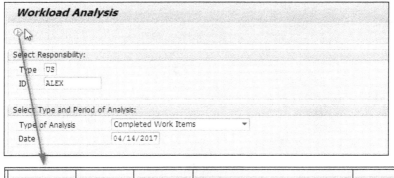

Figure 5.3: Completed work items for single user

The report allows you to run it for a single user, work center, job, organizational unit, or position (see Figure 5.4). The company for the report examples does not use the SAP organizational structure. This, however, does not stop you from taking advantage of the organizational object, WORK CENTER. Create a work center using transaction PO01 and add all the users you want to report on together, see Figure 5.5. This is a subset of the total users who have executed your task.

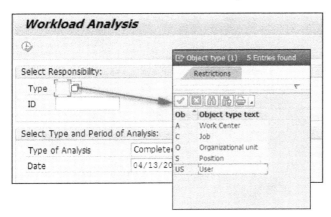

Figure 5.4: Agent types of for reporting

Plan version	Current plan ▼		
Work Center	50001848	Accounts Payable Processor	
Abbr.	AP_PROCESS...		

Start	End	R..	Rel...	Relat.text	R..	Rel'd obje...	Abbr.	% Rate
05/10/2017	12/31/9999	A	008	Holder	US	LINDA	LINDA	0.00
05/09/2017	12/31/9999	A	008	Holder	US	GLENDA	GLENDA	0.00
05/07/2017	12/31/9999	A	008	Holder	US	DANIEL	DANIEL	0.00
05/07/2017	12/31/9999	A	008	Holder	US	JOHN	JOHN	0.00
05/07/2017	12/31/9999	A	008	Holder	US	TONY	TONY	0.00

Figure 5.5: Work center relationships, holders

The report uses the evaluation path WF_ORGUS (t-code OOAW) to resolve HR organizational objects to users. Before you can report with your work center, you must make an additional entry in the SAP delivered evaluation path. Figure 5.6 shows the sequence numbers 10 through 70 that are delivered by SAP. None of these include a path from work center to user. It is expecting personnel numbers to be assigned and then the users will be found by their association with the personnel ID. By adding sequence number 80, you can now use the work center to find your agents. Figure 5.7 reports on the users in the work center you just created.

Change View "Evaluation paths": Overview

New Entries

Dialog Structure	EvalPath	Info	Evaluation path text
▼ Evaluation paths	WF_ORGUN	i	Organizational unit of a user/person (module id Ben./Pers.)
· Evaluation path (indi	WF_ORGUS	i	All users for an object of type A, C, O, S, or US
· Short names	WF_O_TTS	i	All single-step tasks in org. unit environment

Dialog Structure			Evaluation Path	WF_ORGUS All users for an object of type A, C, O, S, or US			
▼ Evaluation paths							
· Evaluation path (indi							
· Short names	No.	Obj. t...	A/B	Relnship	Relationship name	Priority	Rel.obj.type
	10	O	B	002	Is line supervisor of	*	O
	20	O	B	003	Incorporates	*	S
	30	C	A	007	Describes	*	S
	40	A	A	003	Belongs to	*	S
	50	S	A	008	Holder	*	US
	60	S	A	008	Holder	*	P
	70	P	B	208	Is identical to	*	US
	80	A	A	008	Holder	*	US

Figure 5.6: Evaluation path WF_ORGUS, t-code OOAW

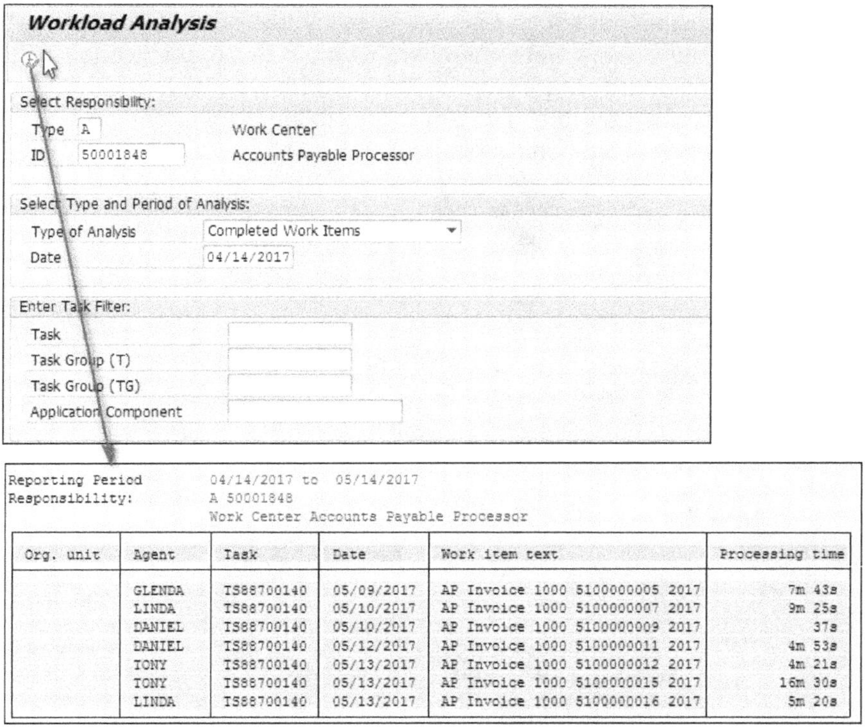

Figure 5.7: Workload analysis based on work center

Work item statistics

SAP evaluates work item execution times using threshold values. As shown in Figure 5.8, there are barriers of 10%, 50%, and 90%. These barriers can also be described as P10, P50, or P90, where P stands for percentile.

When you first run the report for completed work items, you will see a list of all the work items that match your criteria and the processing time of each. You can double click any row and be taken directly to the work item. You can single click on any of the first four columns: ORG. UNIT, AGENT, TASK, or DATE and then click on the Statistics button to see the barriers broken down by that unit.

The HR organizational structure is not used by this example company. If it was and your agents were members of multiple organizational units, you could single click anywhere in the ORG. UNIT column and click on STATISTICS to see how the different organizational units compared. Instead, the organizational unit is blank.

Completed work items by agent and task

⏶ ▼ (Statistics)

Reporting Period   05/01/2017 to 05/13/2017

Org. unit	Agent	Task	Date	Work item text	Processing time
	ALEX	TS88700140	05/09/2017	AP Invoice 1000 5100000002 2017	3m 33s
	ANABELLA	TS88700140	05/09/2017	AP Invoice 1000 5100000005 2017	7m 02s
	GLENDA	TS88700140	05/09/2017	AP Invoice 1000 5100000005 2017	7m 43s
	LINDA	TS88700140	05/10/2017	AP Invoice 1000 5100000007 2017	9m 25s
	DANIEL	TS88700140	05/10/2017	AP Invoice 1000 5100000009 2017	37s
	ALEX	TS88700140	05/12/2017	AP Invoice 1000 5100000010 2017	1m 11s
	DANIEL	TS88700140	05/12/2017	AP Invoice 1000 5100000011 2017	4m 53s
	TONY	TS88700140	05/13/2017	AP Invoice 1000 5100000012 2017	4m 21s
	ALEX	TS88700140	05/13/2017	AP Invoice 1000 5100000013 2017	3m 28s
	ANABELLA	TS88700140	05/13/2017	AP Invoice 1000 5100000014 2017	2m 03s
	TONY	TS88700140	05/13/2017	AP Invoice 1000 5100000015 2017	16m 30s
	LINDA	TS88700140	05/13/2017	AP Invoice 1000 5100000016 2017	5m 20s

Reporting Period   05/01/2017 to 05/13/2017

Agent	Number	10% barrier	50% barrier	90% barrier
ALEX	3	1m 38s	3m 28s	3m 32s
ANABELLA	2	2m 33s	4m 33s	6m 32s
DANIEL	2	1m 03s	2m 45s	4m 27s
GLENDA	1	7m 43s	7m 43s	7m 43s
LINDA	2	5m 45s	7m 23s	9m 01s
TONY	2	5m 34s	10m 26s	15m 17s

Figure 5.8: Percentile breakdown by agent

Figure 5.8 shows an evaluation at the user or agent level. There are six agents who have processed twelve AP invoices. Anabella processed two invoices with times of 7 minutes and 2 seconds and 2 minutes and 3 seconds. The report shows that 10% of the time she will process an invoice in 2 minutes and 33 seconds or less, 50% of the time she will process an invoice in 4 minutes and 33 seconds or less, and 90% of the time she will process an invoice in 6 minutes and 32 seconds or less.

Agent	Number	10% barrier	50% barrier	90% barrier
ANABELLA	2	2m 33s	4m 33s	6m 32s

You may also view the percentile breakdown by task, in Figure 5.9 the 10%, 50%, and 90% barriers for all the work items of the same task are shown. Note that only one task was selected for analysis. You can group several similar tasks together in a task group and compare them here.

Figure 5.9: Percentile breakdown by task

Figure 5.10 shows the breakdown by date. This can be very useful to pinpoint low production days. For example, no work items were processed on Thursday, 5/11/2017. This date could be further investigated to understand why no work items were processed.

133

Completed work items by agent and task

Statistics

Reporting Period   05/01/2017 to 05/13/2017

Org. unit	Agent	Task	Date	Work item text	Processing time
	ALEX	TS88700140	05/09/2017	AP Invoice 1000 5100000002 2017	3m 33s
	ANABELLA	TS88700140	05/09/2017	AP Invoice 1000 5100000005 2017	7m 02s
	GLENDA	TS88700140	05/09/2017	AP Invoice 1000 5100000005 2017	7m 43s
	LINDA	TS88700140	05/10/2017	AP Invoice 1000 5100000007 2017	9m 25s
	DANIEL	TS88700140	05/10/2017	AP Invoice 1000 5100000009 2017	37s
	ALEX	TS88700140	05/12/2017	AP Invoice 1000 5100000010 2017	1m 11s
	DANIEL	TS88700140	05/12/2017	AP Invoice 1000 5100000011 2017	4m 53s
	TONY	TS88700140	05/13/2017	AP Invoice 1000 5100000012 2017	4m 21s
	ALEX	TS88700140	05/13/2017	AP Invoice 1000 5100000013 2017	3m 28s
	ANABELLA	TS88700140	05/13/2017	AP Invoice 1000 5100000014 2017	2m 03s
	TONY	TS88700140	05/13/2017	AP Invoice 1000 5100000015 2017	16m 30s
	LINDA	TS88700140	05/13/2017	AP Invoice 1000 5100000016 2017	5m 20s

Reporting Period   05/01/2017 to 05/13/2017

Date	Number	10% barrier	50% barrier	90% barrier
05/09/2017	3	4m 15s	7m 02s	7m 35s
05/10/2017	2	1m 30s	5m 01s	8m 32s
05/12/2017	2	1m 33s	3m 02s	4m 31s
05/13/2017	5	2m 37s	4m 21s	12m 02s

Figure 5.10: Percentile breakdown by date

5.1.2   Work item to be completed

Running the workload analysis report to see the work items to be completed gives you a way to see what work items are ready to be processed in any user's SAP Business Workplace. Of course, you can also run it to view the work items ready to be processed for an organizational unit, position, job, or work center.

Figure 5.11 shows the work items that have been reserved by Brenda. This means that Brenda has either reserved it from her business workplace or she has executed it but did not complete processing. The other work items are in the section NOT RESERVED BY AN AGENT. This means that Brenda is one of potentially multiple agents who have this work item in their inbox. Brenda is a responsible agent of all the tasks listed (see Section 1.1 for the definition of a responsible agent).

The tasks are grouped into folders. Expand a folder and you can drill into any work item. Regardless of the view you have selected in your personal workflow settings—user view, classic user view, or classical technical view—you can view the selected agents of the work item by going to GO TO • AGENTS.

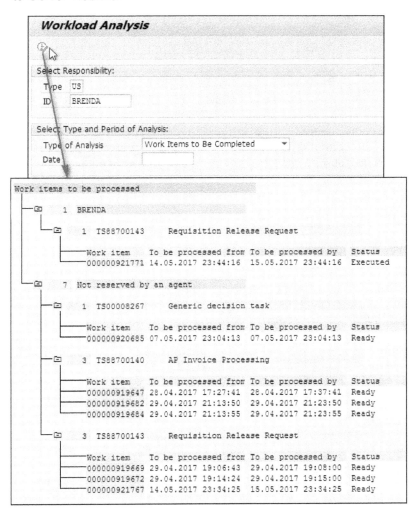

Figure 5.11: Work items to be completed

Task groups for reporting

 Create a task group for tasks that you like to report on often. Many workflow reports have the same task filter selection group which allows the selection of one task, a task group, or an application component.

Task filter	
Task	
Task group (T)	
Task group (TG)	
Application Component	

Because you cannot enter more than one task at a time, if you create a task group you can report on all the tasks you would like to see at the same time.

5.2 Work items without agents

To find the work items without agents report, go to SAP MENU • TOOLS • BUSINESS WORKFLOW • DEVELOPMENT • ADMINISTRATION • WORKFLOW RUNTIME • WORK ITEMS WITHOUT AGENTS or use transaction SWI2_ADM1.

Run this report to see if there are any problems with your workflow definitions finding agents. Figure 5.12 shows the report results based on running SWI2_ADM1 for all tasks. Running the report this way gives the workflow administrator an idea which tasks tend to have agent determination problems.

The workflow administrator will want to investigate the way responsible agents are determined for these workflow tasks and find out what is missing. Say, for example, the workflow administrator investigates the agent determination for work item 919664, REQUISITION 10002034 RELEASE REQUEST. The administrator finds out that the rule first looks to see the cost center owner used on the requisition. In the example scenario, if no cost center is assigned to the requisition or if the cost center owner does not have the appropriate authorization to release the requisition, the agent rule will read the release procedure configuration for finding a workflow agent. In work item 919664's case, the workflow administrator found that the cost center owner did not have the appropriate authorization for the value of the requisition. In cases like this, the release procedure configuration is used to find an agent as a failsafe. However, there was no configuration for the release code of the requisition. The administrator will contact the person responsible for maintaining the release procedure configuration, so the missing entry can be corrected.

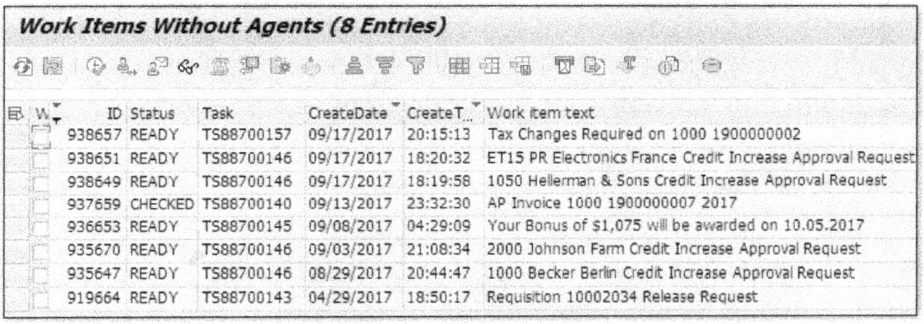
Work Items Without Agents (8 Entries)

ID	Status	Task	CreateDate	CreateT...	Work item text
938657	READY	TS88700157	09/17/2017	20:15:13	Tax Changes Required on 1000 1900000002
938651	READY	TS88700146	09/17/2017	18:20:32	ET15 PR Electronics France Credit Increase Approval Request
938649	READY	TS88700146	09/17/2017	18:19:58	1050 Hellerman & Sons Credit Increase Approval Request
937659	CHECKED	TS88700140	09/13/2017	23:32:30	AP Invoice 1000 1900000007 2017
936653	READY	TS88700145	09/08/2017	04:29:09	Your Bonus of $1,075 will be awarded on 10.05.2017
935670	READY	TS88700146	09/03/2017	21:08:34	2000 Johnson Farm Credit Increase Approval Request
935647	READY	TS88700146	08/29/2017	20:44:47	1000 Becker Berlin Credit Increase Approval Request
919664	READY	TS88700143	04/29/2017	18:50:17	Requisition 10002034 Release Request

Figure 5.12: Work items without agents

Once the configuration entry is created for the requisition's release code, the workflow administrator will be told, and they can rerun the agent rule for this work item. It is necessary to rerun the rule because the rule is only executed when the work item is first created. Figure 5.13 shows how the administrator will select the work item that needs its rule rerun and will click on the EXECUTE AGENT RULES icon to have the rule run again. Note: multiple work items can be selected and have all their rules be rerun at the same time. The administrator will then refresh the report and if rerunning the rule was successful, the work item will be removed from the report.

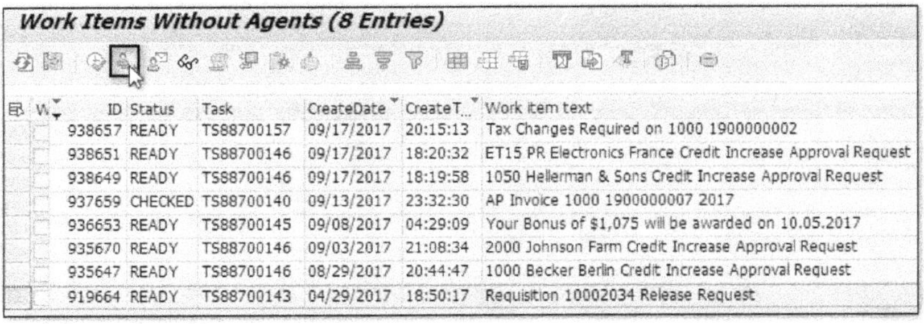
Work Items Without Agents (8 Entries)

ID	Status	Task	CreateDate	CreateT...	Work item text
938657	READY	TS88700157	09/17/2017	20:15:13	Tax Changes Required on 1000 1900000002
938651	READY	TS88700146	09/17/2017	18:20:32	ET15 PR Electronics France Credit Increase Approval Request
938649	READY	TS88700146	09/17/2017	18:19:58	1050 Hellerman & Sons Credit Increase Approval Request
937659	CHECKED	TS88700140	09/13/2017	23:32:30	AP Invoice 1000 1900000007 2017
936653	READY	TS88700145	09/08/2017	04:29:09	Your Bonus of $1,075 will be awarded on 10.05.2017
935670	READY	TS88700146	09/03/2017	21:08:34	2000 Johnson Farm Credit Increase Approval Request
935647	READY	TS88700146	08/29/2017	20:44:47	1000 Becker Berlin Credit Increase Approval Request
919664	READY	TS88700143	04/29/2017	18:50:17	Requisition 10002034 Release Request

Figure 5.13: Execute agent rules

Not all work items use a rule to determine responsible agents. Consider work item 938657, TAX CHANGES REQUIRED ON 1000 1900000002. This work item is for a task that has the possible agents defined as a role (see Figure 5.14). The workflow task behind this same work item has the responsible agents defined as an organizational unit (see Figure 5.15). The agents of organizational unit 50028925 do not include the one user assigned to the task's role, Donna. Because of this, work item 938657 appears on the list of WORK ITEMS WITHOUT AGENTS (see Figure 5.16). The workflow administrator will alert the functional team that the assignments need to be corrected. Once the functional team corrects the assignments, the workflow administrator will click on the EXECUTE AGENT RULES icon and the work item will be removed from the report.

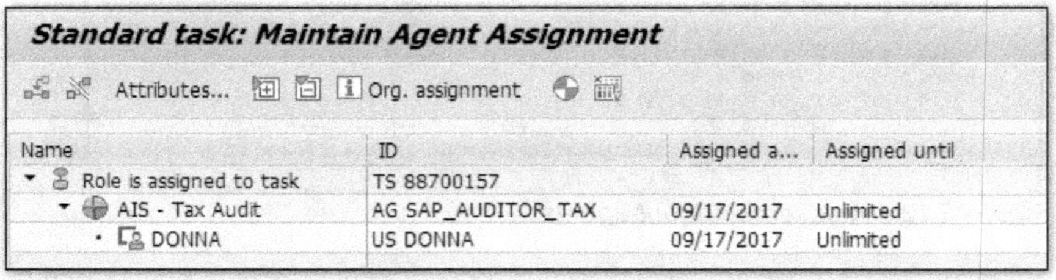
Standard task: Maintain Agent Assignment
Attributes...
Org. assignment
Name
ID
Assigned a...
Assigned until
Role is assigned to task
TS 88700157
AIS - Tax Audit
AG SAP_AUDITOR_TAX
09/17/2017
Unlimited
DONNA
US DONNA
09/17/2017
Unlimited

Figure 5.14: Possible agents defined as a role

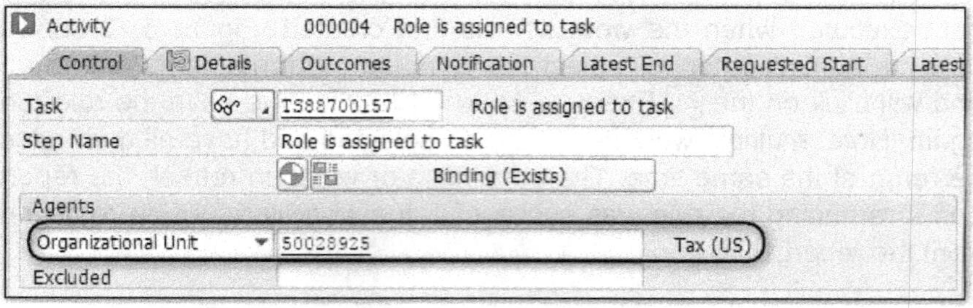
Activity
000004 Role is assigned to task
Control
Details
Outcomes
Notification
Latest End
Requested Start
Latest
Task
TS88700157
Role is assigned to task
Step Name
Role is assigned to task
Binding (Exists)
Agents
Organizational Unit
50028925
Tax (US)
Excluded

Figure 5.15: Responsible agents assigned as an organizational unit

Work Items Without Agents (8 Entries)

	W	ID	Status	Task	CreateDate	CreateT...	Work item text
		938657	READY	TS88700157	09/17/2017	20:35:38	Tax Changes Required on 1000 1900000002
		938651	READY	TS88700146	09/17/2017	18:20:32	ET15 PR Electronics France Credit Increase Approval Request
		938649	READY	TS88700146	09/17/2017	18:19:58	1050 Hellerman & Sons Credit Increase Approval Request
		937659	CHECKED	TS88700140	09/13/2017	23:32:30	AP Invoice 1000 1900000007 2017
		936653	READY	TS88700145	09/08/2017	04:29:09	Your Bonus of $1,075 will be awarded on 10.05.2017
		935670	READY	TS88700146	09/03/2017	21:08:34	2000 Johnson Farm Credit Increase Approval Request
		935647	READY	TS88700146	08/29/2017	20:44:47	1000 Becker Berlin Credit Increase Approval Request

Figure 5.16: No agent found for task with role agent assignment

Streamline error handling

 The two examples in this section illustrate the benefit of using a functional person as a workflow-specific administrator. In both cases, the workflow administrator discovers the problem and then must turn to functional IT people to solve the agent problem. The functional person then must get back with the workflow administrator to have the work item agent rules rerun. Why not design the workflow in a way that it will produce an error if no agent is found and set up a functional IT person as a workflow-specific administrator? Or, if you don't want to set a functional person as the workflow administrator, you can always design the roles so that if no one is found, a functional IT person will become the agent. When the functional IT person receives the work item, they will know there is an agent assignment problem and they can correct the problem. In the meantime, they can simply forward the work item they received to the appropriate recipient without having to get the workflow administrator's help to rerun the agent rules.

5.3 Work items with deleted users

To find the report for items with deleted user, go to SAP MENU • TOOLS • BUSINESS WORKFLOW • DEVELOPMENT • ADMINISTRATION • WORKFLOW RUNTIME • WORK ITEMS WITHOUT AGENTS or use transaction SWI2_ADM2, see Figure 5.17.

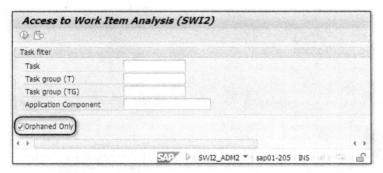

Figure 5.17: Work items with deleted users

Run this report to see if there have been any work items with deleted users or if there are any orphaned work items. This happens when a work item is assigned agents, but before the work item is processed, the assigned agents' SAP user IDs are deleted or delimited.

SWI2_ADM2 can be run to show all the work items that have deleted users, or it can be run with the option, ORPHANED ONLY to see the orphaned work items. A work item may have deleted users as agents, but may still have other users who are valid agents of the task. A work item is considered orphaned if all SAP user IDs assigned to it are invalid.

Delimited vs. deleted

 It is not a good practice to delete users, rather, users should be delimited, e.g. be given an end date. Work items for users who have a valid end date delimited prior to the current date rather than deleted will not show up on the WORK ITEMS WITHOUT AGENTS report (see Section 5.2). A delimited user is a user who remains in the system but can no longer log on the system because their valid end date expired.

You can run the WORKLOAD ANALYSIS report, transaction SWI5. See Section 5.1.2 for more information on finding work items to be completed for a user. This will only work for users who are delimited, not deleted. Figure 5.18 shows the error message you will receive if you try and run SWI5 for a deleted user. If the user is delimited, when running SWI5 you will receive a warning that the user is only valid for the user's validity dates. After you acknowledge the warning, you can view the work items assigned.

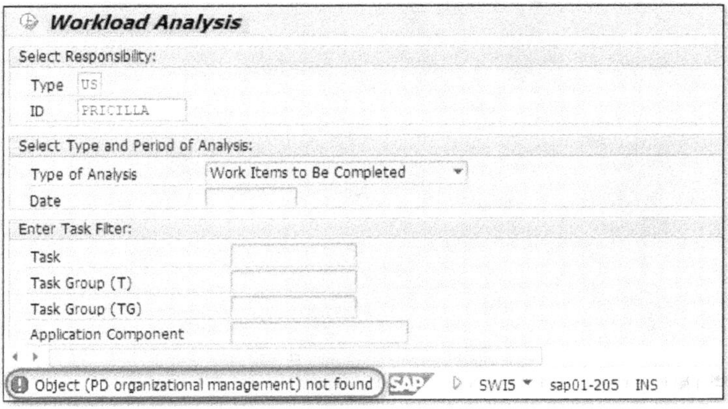

Figure 5.18: Workload analysis cannot be run for deleted users

5.4   Work items with monitored deadlines

To find the report of work items with monitored deadlines, go to SAP MENU • TOOLS • BUSINESS WORKFLOW • DEVELOPMENT • ADMINISTRATION • WORKFLOW RUNTIME • WORK ITEMS WITH MONITORED DEADLINES or use transaction SWI2_DEAD.

If any workflow definitions take advantage of SAP's monitored deadlines, as shown in Section 1.3, you can use this report to see which work items have been placed in deadline status. This report is a good tool for finding bottlenecks in your workflow processes. If there is a task that routinely goes into deadline status, this may indicate a need for the workflow definition to be redesigned. Maybe more users could become agents of the task so that more people have an opportunity to perform the task before

141

it goes into deadline status; maybe the task could be rewritten so that it is less time consuming for the agent to execute.

A requirement for deadlines to occur is to have the background job for missed deadlines running (see Figure 5.19). The default time interval at which the background job is called is every three minutes. With each execution, the background job checks whether new deadlines have been missed since the last time it ran. This means that the deadline work item will not be sent out at the exact time that the deadline was reached. It will be sent once the deadline is reached plus the amount of time remaining until the deadline job runs again, which will be up to three minutes.

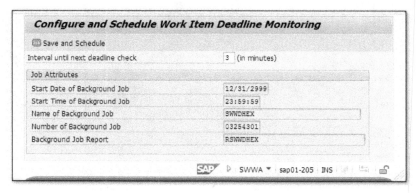

Figure 5.19: T-code SWWA to configure deadline monitoring job

5.5 Diagnosis of workflows with errors

To find the report to diagnose workflows with errors, go to SAP MENU • TOOLS • BUSINESS WORKFLOW • DEVELOPMENT • ADMINISTRATION • WORK-FLOW RUNTIME • DIAGNOSIS OF WORKFLOWS WITH ERRORS or use transaction SWI2_DIAG.

The DIAGNOSIS OF WORKFLOWS WITH ERRORS REPORT has been run as shown in Figure 5.20. This report shows multiple error types, including errors that have nothing to do with agent determination. Take a closer look at work item 921758 (see Figure 5.21). This error is a result of a rule that is configured to error if no agent is found (see Figure 3.9).

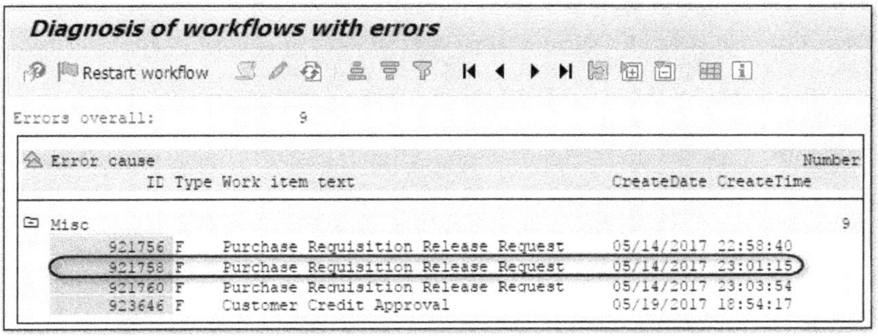

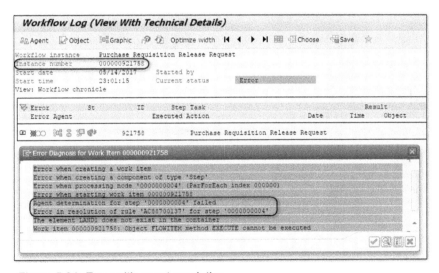

Figure 5.20: Diagnosis of workflows with errors

Figure 5.21: Error with agent resolution

6 Agent administration

The most dynamic aspect of any workflow is the agent assignment. For example, employees are hired, terminated, and they retire. Contractors may be employed temporarily to handle large workloads and then leave. Employees change positions, are promoted, and they transfer from location to location within the company. Because of these changes in personnel, errors pertaining to agents might be the most frequent of all the issues a workflow administrator will address.

There are two types of workflow administrators: the global workflow administrator and the workflow-specific administrator. Global administrators can be defined as a role, organizational unit, job, position, work center, user, or rule. Keep in mind if you define this as a rule there is no way to populate a rule container. Workflow-specific administrators can be defined with even more flexibility. See Figure 2.16 for the ways a workflow-specific administrator may be defined.

Global workflow administrator

The global workflow administrator, defined via transaction SWU3 (see Figure 6.1), is notified when a workflow instance encounters an error, unless the workflow definition has a workflow-specific administrator defined. Usually the global workflow administrator(s) will be technical because they will encounter technical errors, not just errors associated with missing agents.

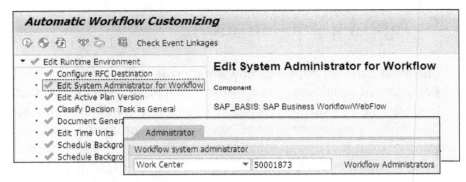

Figure 6.1: Transaction SWU3 global workflow administrator

Use a role to define the global workflow administrator

 Assign the workflow administrator via a PFTC role, e.g., SAP_BC_BMT_WFM_ADMIN. By assigning in this way, you ensure that when someone receives a workflow error message they have authorization to do something about the error. OSS Note 2191614 issued 2013-Sep-27 allows workflow administrator to be assigned with roles.

If there is no role that defines narrowly enough who the workflow administrators should be, build a work center (t-code po01) and add the applicable persons, positions, jobs, or users to this work center. Figure 5.6 shows the required evaluation path changes that need to be made to WF_ORGUS so that the work center can properly resolve to users, if you choose to assign users directly to the work center.

Workflow-specific administrator

To define a workflow-specific administrator, from inside the workflow definition click on the 🖳 icon to go to the header area of the workflow, then click on the VERSION-DEPENDENT tab, and then the AGENTS tab, see Figure 6.2.

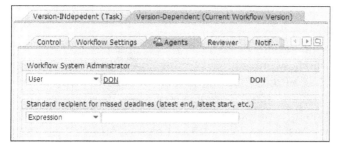

Figure 6.2: Workflow-specific administrator

Bear in mind, being specified as a workflow administrator, either globally or workflow-specific, does not give someone authorization to perform any workflow administrative tasks. Each workflow administrator must have the appropriate security roles assigned to them (see Figure 6.9).

If you would like to find out all the workflow definitions that have a workflow administrator assigned, read table SWDSEXPR with field EXPRTYPE = 16 (see Figure 6.3).

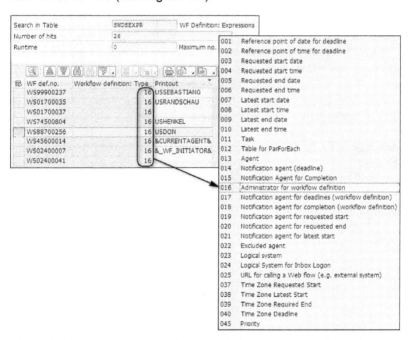

Figure 6.3: Table SWDSEXPR holds workflow-specific administrator

Use the workflow-specific administrator functionality

It is a good practice to have a functional person close to the workflow process be the first line of defense when a workflow error occurs. If the functional person can solve the problem, that is great, if not, they can forward the error notification on to the global workflow administrator. A functional person will more likely have better information on the process and they may be able to better prioritize the issue and provide appropriate communication to the people involved. Workflow-specific administrator assignment allows functional agents to be assigned to the workflows they know and understand.

6.1 Work item administrator service panel

The focus of this book is on workflow agents so it's time to look at what is available to the workflow administrator for resolving issues that pertain to agents. Dialog and deadline work items are the two types that have agents. There are many activities available to the workflow administrator from within the technical work item. Please refer to the workflow settings, as shown in Figure 6.4, for the work item display and the workflow log display which are used for screen shots for this book. The CLASSIC TECHNICAL VIEW of the workflow log is displayed in Figure 6.5.

There are many paths to the technical work item. From any workflow report or from the SAP Business Workplace, you can click to select a work item and then click on the WORKFLOW LOG icon and be taken to the workflow log for the work item (see Figure 6.6) for getting to the workflow log from SAP Business Workplace.

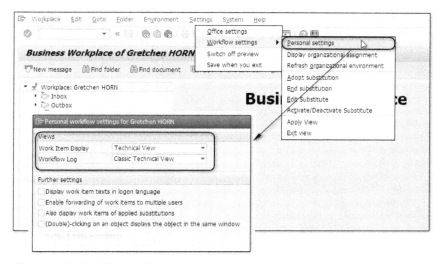

Figure 6.4: Workflow settings

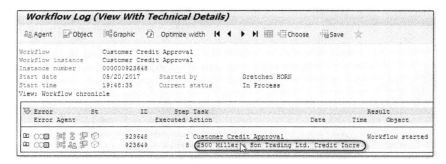

Figure 6.5: Workflow log technical view

Figure 6.6: Go to the workflow log from SAP Business Workplace

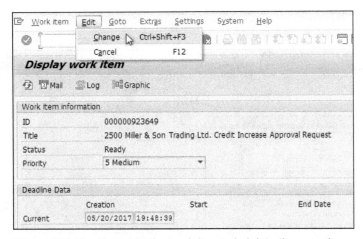

Figure 6.7: How to get to the work item administration panel

From inside the technical work item display go to, EDIT ⇨ CHANGE or EXTRAS ⇨ ACTIVATE ADMINISTRATION to bring up the administration panel, see Figure 6.7.

The activities available on the administration panel (see Figure 6.8) will depend on values assigned to the administrator for the authorization object S_WF_WI (see Figure 6.9). Focus on the administrative activities that effect agent assignment. The list of activities is based on what activities make sense for the state of the work item. For example, a work item with a READY status will not have the MANUALLY REPLACE activity because this activity is not appropriate for the work item based on its status. If a work item is completed, there is not much available for change, but the workflow or task container can be changed from the administrative panel.

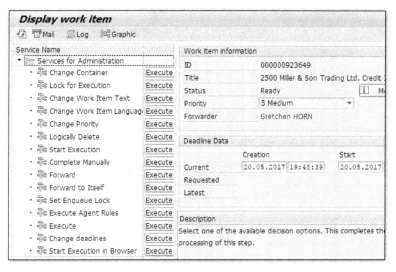

Figure 6.8: Work item administrator service panel

6.1.1 Forward and forward to itself

The easiest way for a workflow administrator to direct a work item to another agent is to forward it to someone. The workflow administrator is not bound by the forwarding rules as described in Section 4.1.1. The workflow administrator may forward a work item to any user, including themselves, if they have the required authorization.

Object	S_WF_WI
Text	Workflow: Work Item Handling
Class	BC_Z Basis - Central Functions
Author	SAP

Authorization fields

Authorization Field Short Description...	
WI_TYPE	Work item type
TASK_CLASS	Classification of Tasks
WFACTVT	Activities for authorization check

Authorization Object Documentation

    Display Object Documentation

Activity	Authorization Value
11	Change deadlines
12	Resubmit work item
13	Administration: Set work item status to "Completed"
14	Administration: Reset work item manually
15	Administration: Set work item status to "Logically Deleted"
16	Start task
17	Administration: Edit Container
18	Administration: Lock/unlock execution
19	Change priority
20	Administration: Change language
21	Administration: Change work item text
22	Administration: Change
23	Choose
24	Administration: Change callback function module (obsolete)
25	Change agent (required for forwarding)
26	Administration: End wait state
27	Administration: Restart after error
28	Administration: Execute
29	Add activity
30	Determine number of work items of other users
31	Administration: Change Workflow Instance Settings
32	Delete deadlines
33	Administration: Set Enqueue Lock
34	Administration: Reset Enqueue Lock
35	Administration: Forward
36	Administration: Execute Conditions
37	Administration: Execute Processing Rule
38	Administration: Cancel manually and continue after error
39	Administration: Change Deadlines (11 additionally required)
40	Edit XML messages
41	Display Technical Container Elements
42	Administration: Set to Done

Figure 6.9: Workflow administrator authorization object

6.1.2 Change deadlines

The administrator may want to change the deadlines to affect when the deadline agents receive their notifications. In the example shown in Figure 6.10, a work item was created at 8:18:38 and was set to go into deadline monitoring status three hours later, at 11:18:13. This time can be changed to any time in the future. In addition, the other deadlines that were not defined in the workflow definition can be set now. Granted, if deadlines were not defined in the workflow definition, the only thing that will happen is that the original agent will see that the work item is in deadline status from their SAP Business Workplace inbox; no notification agent can be added at runtime.

Tip for testing workflows in deadline status

Changing a work item deadline is very useful when test-ing workflows with deadline monitoring. For each test, you can change the timing so that you can, for example, wait 1 minute instead of having to wait a week, or what-ever the defined time is.

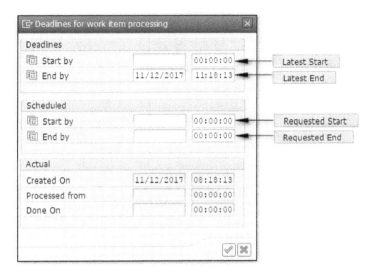

Figure 6.10: Change deadlines

6.1.3 Execute agent rules

From time to time, a workflow administrator may need to re-execute the agent rules, including excluded agents, for a workflow instance. This happens if there is an open work item that uses a rule and the data the rule evaluates is different from when the work item was first instantiated. Notice in Figure 6.11 that the credit rep position S 50009302 is vacant. When this position is filled, if there are any existing work items that have this position as the agent, the work items will need to have their agent rules rerun so the agents for the work item reflect the user who filled the position. See Section 3.4 for information on rules that read organizational data.

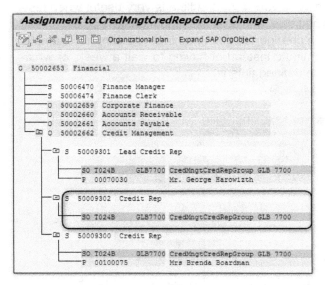

Figure 6.11: Position assigned to T024B is vacant

6.1.4 Lock/unlock for execution

A workflow administrator can toggle a work item from UNLOCK FOR EXECUTION to LOCK FOR EXECUTION. An administrator would want to lock a work item for execution so that it cannot be processed until later.

6.1.5 Replace manually

If a work item has been reserved by someone, it will have the status of SELECTED with a status description of RESERVED. If a work item has been executed and then subsequently cancelled it will have the status of STARTED with the status description of IN PROCESS. If the dialog task has the setting, CONFIRM END OF PROCESSING and must be explicitly ended, instead of the status STARTED, it will have the status COMMITTED. Both STARTED and COMMITTED have the status description of IN PROCESS.

Work items with status of SELECTED or STARTED can be put back into the READY status by being replaced by the acting agent or by a workflow administrator. By setting the work item status back to READY, it is now be visible to all the work item recipients.

Do your users always forget to replace a work item?

 It can be troublesome if a user executes a work item, decides to cancel out of the work item, and then forgets to place it back into the queue. By cancelling the execution of a dialog work item, its status will be set to STARTED or COMMITTED and the work item will be automatically reserved by the user who executed it. Because the work item is now reserved, it is no longer visible to other users who are work item agents. This stalls the processing of work and can cause work items to be processed late. Fortunately, SAP has provided a way to override this functionality. For synchronous dialog tasks, simply add the task number to table SWW_TASKCUST. If a task is configured in this table, all work items of this task will have a status of READY if their execution is cancelled by a user. If a user wants to reserve the work item, the reserve and replace functionality is still available for this task in SAP Business Workplace. Keep in mind, this functionality is task-specific, if a task is used by multiple workflow definitions, the behavior will be changed for all instances of this task. See OSS Note 1676067 for more information on this functionality.

6.2 The workflow administrator's report

To get to the workflow administrator's report, go to SAP MENU • TOOLS • BUSINESS WORKFLOW • DEVELOPMENT • ADMINISTRATION • WORKFLOW RUNTIME • EXECUTE WORK ITEM WITHOUT AGENT CHECK or use transaction SWIA.

This report is actually titled, "Execute work item without agent check," but I don't believe this title does the report justice. Everything that an administrator can do from the technical work item administration panel can be performed from this report. What this report has over the administration panel is that, in some cases, multiple work items can be processed at once.

6.2.1 Process work items without agent check

Even having workflow administrator authorization, the admin must use the correct tool to execute a work item as the administrator. Transaction SWIA is one way a work item can be executed by a workflow administrator. See Figure 6.12 to see the error a workflow administrator receives if trying to execute a work item from another workflow report, e.g. SWI1. Alternatively, Figure 6.13 shows how the workflow administrator can run transaction SWIA and execute work items without check.

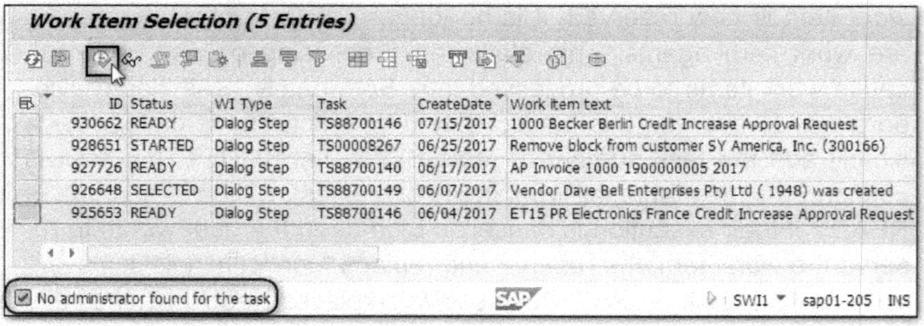

Figure 6.12: No administrator found for the task

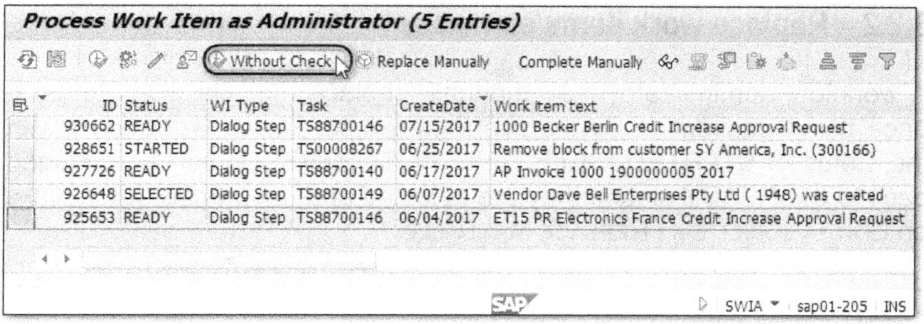

Process Work Item as Administrator (5 Entries)

	ID	Status	WI Type	Task	CreateDate	Work item text
	930662	READY	Dialog Step	TS88700146	07/15/2017	1000 Becker Berlin Credit Increase Approval Request
	928651	STARTED	Dialog Step	TS00008267	06/25/2017	Remove block from customer SY America, Inc. (300166)
	927726	READY	Dialog Step	TS88700140	06/17/2017	AP Invoice 1000 1900000005 2017
	926648	SELECTED	Dialog Step	TS88700149	06/07/2017	Vendor Dave Bell Enterprises Pty Ltd (1948) was created
	925653	READY	Dialog Step	TS88700146	06/04/2017	ET15 PR Electronics France Credit Increase Approval Request

SWIA ▼ sap01-205 INS

Figure 6.13: Execute work item as workflow administrator

Run report SWIA if you want to execute work items as the workflow administrator. There is no agent check; however, there is an audit trail that shows that the work item was executed by the workflow administrator and will show the work item administrator's user ID (see Figure 6.14).

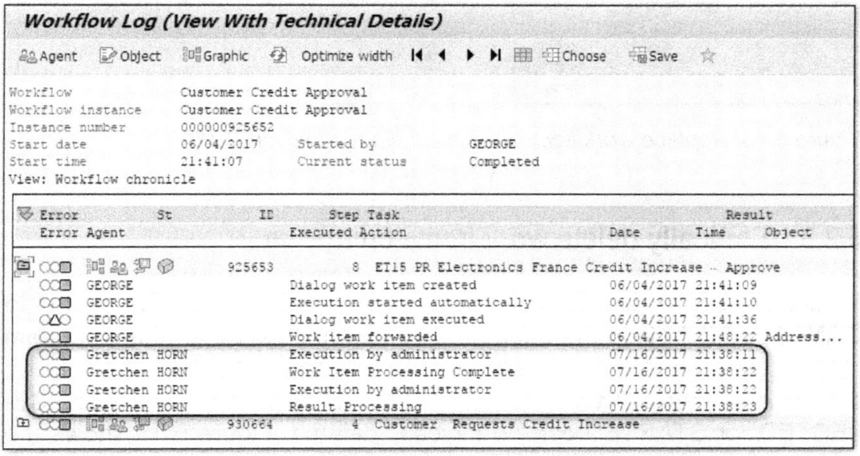

Workflow Log (View With Technical Details)

```
Agent    Object    Graphic    Optimize width  I4  ◀  ▶  ▶I  ⊞  Choose   Save   ☆

Workflow               Customer Credit Approval
Workflow instance      Customer Credit Approval
Instance number        000000925652
Start date             06/04/2017      Started by          GEORGE
Start time             21:41:07        Current status      Completed
View: Workflow chronicle
```

Error	St	ID	Step Task			Result	
Error Agent			Executed Action	Date	Time	Object	
⬚ ☐☐☐		925653	8 ET15 PR Electronics France Credit Increase – Approve				
☐☐☐ GEORGE			Dialog work item created	06/04/2017	21:41:09	
☐☐☐ GEORGE			Execution started automatically	06/04/2017	21:41:10	
☐△☐ GEORGE			Dialog work item executed	06/04/2017	21:41:36	
☐☐☐ GEORGE			Work item forwarded	06/04/2017	21:48:22	Address...
☐☐☐ Gretchen HORN			Execution by administrator	07/16/2017	21:38:11	
☐☐☐ Gretchen HORN			Work Item Processing Complete	07/16/2017	21:38:22	
☐☐☐ Gretchen HORN			Execution by administrator	07/16/2017	21:38:22	
☐☐☐ Gretchen HORN			Result Processing	07/16/2017	21:38:23	
☐☐ ☐☐☐		930664	4 Customer Requests Credit Increase				

Figure 6.14: Audit trail workflow administrator executing work item

6.2.2   Replace work items en masse

A workflow administrator may manually replace multiple work items at once using transaction SWIA, see Figure 6.15. Dialog work items with the status of STARTED, SELECTED, or COMMITTED can be changed back to the READY state if they are selected and the administrator clicks on EDIT • WORK ITEM • REPLACE MANUALLY.

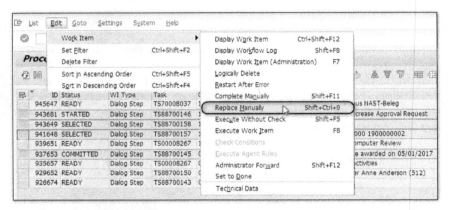

Figure 6.15: Replace work items en masse via transaction SWIA

6.2.3   Logically delete work items en masse

By completing a work item manually, you will be changing the status to CANCELLED, having the description DELETED LOGICALLY. The work item status cannot be ERROR, CANCELLED, or COMPLETED. Work items that have a status of WAITING, READY, COMMITTED, CHECKED, SE-LECTED, or STARTED can be logically deleted. Figure 6.16 shows the action of logically deleting the selected work items from transaction SWIA. Figure 6.17 shows the status of these logically deleted work items as CANCELLED.

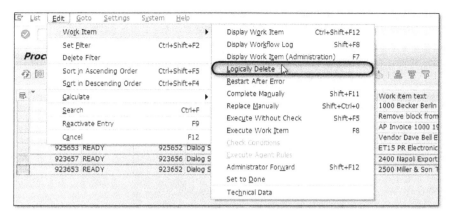

Figure 6.16: Logically delete work items en masse

Figure 6.17: Work items set to CANCELLED when logically deleted

6.2.4 Manually complete work items

From transaction SWIA, the administrator can select one work item and click on COMPLETE MANUALLY, see Figure 6.18. The administrator will select from a list of available outcomes for the task, see Figure 6.19. This function cannot be performed en masse because an outcome must be selected for each work item. Many times, executing a work item will result in changes to the work item's container elements. The administrator will have to take care to make the appropriate changes to the container for the outcome that was selected.

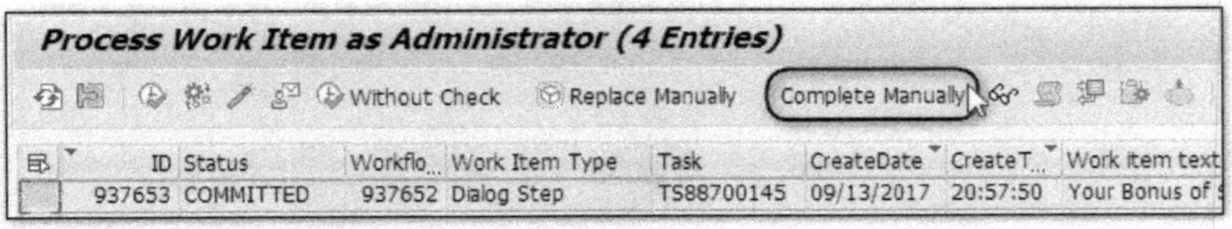

Figure 6.18: Transaction SWIA

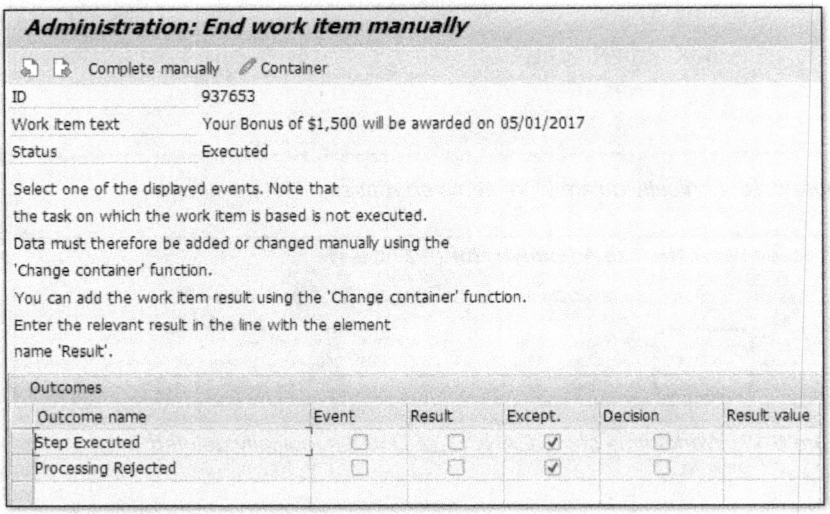

Figure 6.19: End work item manually

6.3   Substitution

This section focuses on transaction RMPS_SET_SUBSTITUTE. Substitution by individual users is described in Section 4.4. Additionally, the workflow administrator can set up active or passive substitution for other users or positions of other users, see Figure 6.20. From transaction RMPS_SET_SUBSTITUTE, the administrator will enter the SAP user ID for whom they want to set up substitutes. Similar to when a user sets up a substitute for themselves, if they set up passive substitution the substitute will still need to accept the substitution from their SAP Business Workplace. The administrator can click on SUBSTITUTES FOR POSITIONS and be presented with the position(s) assigned to the user. They can set up substitutes for this position. Alternatively, if they know the position they want to make a substitution for, instead of the SAP user ID, they may set up the *HR substitution relationship 210* from transaction po01 for the position. See Section 8.1.4 of the appendix for an example.

Figure 6.20: Substitution setup by administrator

Behind the scenes

Find out who in your company is taking advantage of substitution. See the substitute section in the appendix, 8.1.4 to find the tables used for workflow substitution. From the tables, you can quickly see who is using substitutes and those who are acting as substitutes.

6.4   Execute rules for work items

To find the functionality to execute rules for work items, go to SAP MENU • TOOLS • BUSINESS WORKFLOW • DEVELOPMENT • ADMINISTRATION • WORK-FLOW RUNTIME • EXECUTE RULES FOR WORK ITEMS or use transaction SWI1_RULE.

The functionality of re-executing agent rules is described in Section 6.1.3. Because it can be performed from the work item log, it may make more sense to perform this action from a report so that all work items can be processed en masse. You would want to do this after organizational data or responsibilities are updated. It is safer to rerun all the open tasks that are affected by the change so that none are missed.

6.5   Rule simulation

Simulating a rule is a very useful tool to the workflow administrator. Once a work item has been completed, the selected agents are no longer visible, unless the rule result was specifically collected. If it is necessary to know who the agents are for a combination of container elements, rule simulation can be used. Rule simulation is performed using transaction PFAC.

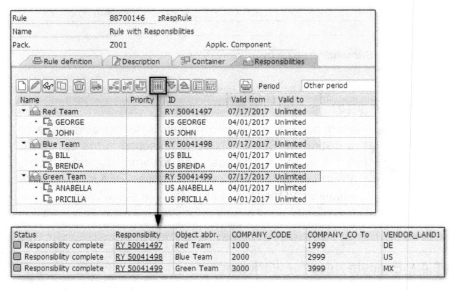

Figure 6.21: Rule responsibility definition used for rule simulation

To simulate this rule with responsibilities, click on the SIMULATION icon as shown in Figure 6.22. You must provide values to the container elements. ❶ in Figure 6.23 shows the test of company code 1025 and vendor country DE. The result is agents George and John. ❷ in Figure 6.23 uses different values which result in different agents. This handy tool will allow an administrator to see if any agents are returned for a particular data combination. The rule simulation is based on a rule with responsibilities, as shown in Figure 6.21.

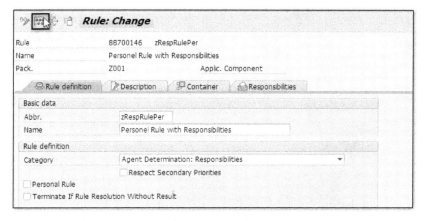

Figure 6.22: Simulate a rule with responsibilities

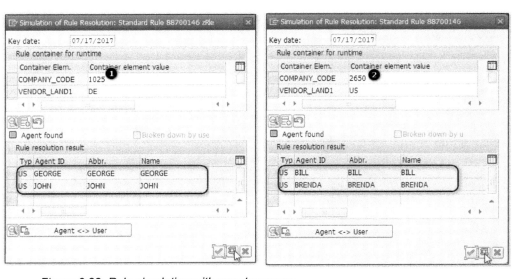

Figure 6.23: Rule simulation with agent success

7 Workshops

7.1 Rule with responsibilities using priorities

A very common use of priorities is for finding a default agent or adminis-trator if the higher priority responsibilities do not return an agent. When priorities are used in this manner, it is to avoid having a work item error because no agent is found, followed by a message going to the workflow administrator. Instead of receiving a message, the default administrator will receive the actual work item and they can forward it to the appropri-ate person. The administrator can then correct the agent assignment problem.

To create a rule with responsibilities using priorities, select the rule cate-gory for responsibilities. When RESPONSIBILITIES is selected, a check box for RESPECT SECONDARY PRIORITIES appears. This check box should be checked (see Figure 7.1).

Figure 7.1: Rule with responsibilities using priorities

To illustrate priorities, you have a very simple rule that assigns one or more managers to a plant. The plants have a numbering scheme where plants that begin with a 1 or a 2 are European plants and plants that begin with a 3 are American plants. Each plant has its own responsibility defined and has a priority of 75.

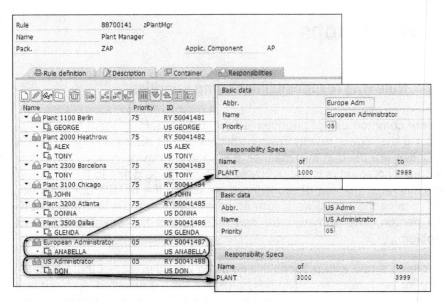

Figure 7.2: Administrators defined with lower priorities

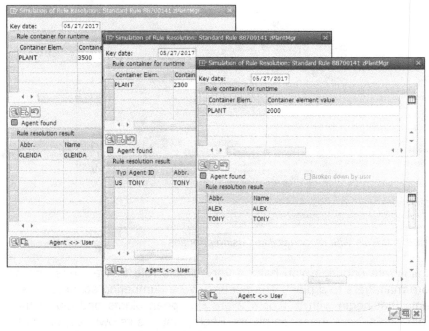

Figure 7.3: Simulation of plants that have responsibilities

Rule: Change

S.	Responsibility	Name	Start date	End Date	PLANT	PLANT To
☐	RY 50041481	Plant 1100 Berlin	05/27/2017	12/31/9999	1100	
☐	RY 50041482	Plant 2000 Heathrow	05/27/2017	12/31/9999	2000	
☐	RY 50041483	Plant 2300 Barcelona	05/27/2017	12/31/9999	2300	
☐	RY 50041484	Plant 3100 Chicago	05/27/2017	12/31/9999	3100	
☐	RY 50041485	Plant 3200 Atlanta	05/27/2017	12/31/9999	3200	
☐	RY 50041486	Plant 3500 Dallas	05/27/2017	12/31/9999	3500	
☐	RY 50041487	European Administrator	05/27/2017	12/31/9999	1000	2999
☐	RY 50041488	US Administrator	05/27/2017	12/31/9999	3000	3999

Figure 7.4: Responsibility definition

Figure 7.4 shows the plants assigned to each responsibility. The plant-specific responsibilities have a higher priority and are assigned only one plant. The responsibilities that have ranges of plants assigned will have a lower priority and will only be used if there is no plant-specific responsibility for a plant in that range, see Figure 7.2.

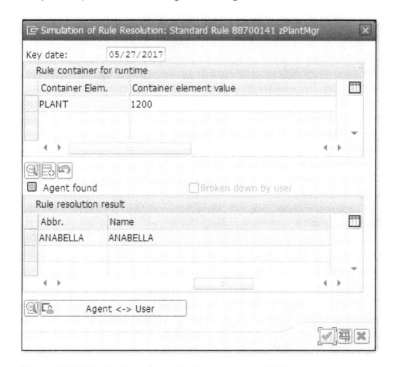

Figure 7.5: Simulation of plant with no responsibility

167

Priorities allow the rule to be read multiple times; if reading the highest priority responsibilities does not return agents, the rule will be read again for all the responsibilities with the next-highest priority, and so on. Figure 7.3 shows how the appropriate plant manager is found when a plant that has a responsibility defined is used. A new plant in Dresden, plant 1200, comes online and there is not yet a responsibility created for it. Figure 7.5 shows how the lower-priority European administrator is found as the agent.

Rule	88700140	zLANGU_COMP
Name	Company Code by Language	
Pack.	ZAP	Applic. Component	AP

Rule definition   Description   Container   Responsibilities

Period   Other period

Name	Priority	ID	Assigned a...	Assigned u...
Company 1000 Fluent English	90	RY 50041472		
· BRENDA		US BRENDA	05/27/2017	07/01/2017
· TRACI		US TRACI	05/27/2017	07/15/2017
Company 1000 Conversational English	50	RY 50041474		
· GARY		US GARY	05/27/2017	Unlimited
Company 1000 Fluent Spanish	90	RY 50041475		
· BILL		US BILL	05/27/2017	Unlimited
· PRICILLA		US PRICILLA	05/27/2017	Unlimited
Company 1000 Conversational Spanish	50	RY 50041476		
· GLENDA		US GLENDA	05/27/2017	Unlimited
Company 2000 Fluent English	90	RY 50041477		
· ALEX		US ALEX	05/27/2017	Unlimited
· GEORGE		US GEORGE	05/27/2017	Unlimited
· JENNIFER		US JENNIFER	05/27/2017	Unlimited
Company 2000 Conversational English	50	RY 50041478		
· JOHN		US JOHN	05/27/2017	Unlimited
· LINDA		US LINDA	05/27/2017	Unlimited
Company 2000 Fluent Spanish	90	RY 50041479		
· DON		US DON	05/27/2017	Unlimited
· DONNA		US DONNA	05/27/2017	Unlimited
Company 2000 Conversational Spanish	50	RY 50041480		
· ANABELLA		US ANABELLA	05/27/2017	Unlimited
· DANIEL		US DANIEL	05/27/2017	Unlimited
· TONY		US TONY	05/27/2017	Unlimited

Figure 7.6: Priorities based on language aptitude

Another use for priorities is to distinguish the best agents for the work vs. agents who will pass if the best agents are not available. This sounds harsh, but consider language aptitude. Some people may speak a language fluently and others may have a conversational aptitude for a language, as opposed to fluent. You want agents for your work item to be fluent in the work item's language, but if a fluent agent is not available, you would like to have someone who can speak the language at least conversationally. Figure 7.6 shows a rule that has responsibilities prioritized by language ability. Responsibilities with the description of fluent are prioritized at level 90, higher than priority level 50, the priority of responsibilities with the description of conversational.

Notice that Brenda and Traci are both scheduled to be removed as agents of responsibility for fluent English by mid-July. If a work item that uses this rule is created, say in August 2017, Brenda and Traci will no longer be valid agents and therefore the secondary priority level 50 for company 1000, language English, will be used and Gary will be the agent. Figure 7.7 shows in the second frame with the KEY DATE of 07/25/2017 that the agent found is GARY. This is because the key date is past the validity period of both Brenda and Traci.

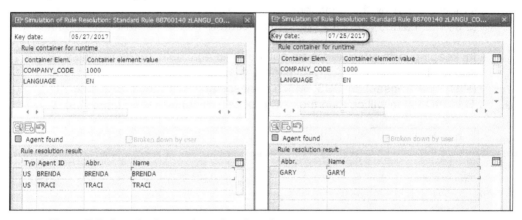

Figure 7.7: Agents change based on key date

7.2 Rule that reads BRF+ rule engine

You can create very robust rules using SAP Business Rule Framework Plus (BRF+). In Section 3.5, you built a rule that calls a BRF+ function which reads a BRF+ decision table. In this workshop, you will build a rule that reads a BRF+ ruleset, which in turn will access multiple BRF+ objects (e.g. decision tables, decision trees, database lookups, etc.) to obtain the agents.

7.2.1 Scenario

Return to the accounts payable scenario. The company is comprised of two global business units. You have global centralized AP processing centers on multiple continents that process invoices for both business units. You want the rule to take advantage of the existing roles in the system, so it will not be necessary to manually link the AP processors to their business unit (e.g. you want to avoid having to maintain the relationship of AP processor and business unit using responsibilities).

Invoices will be scanned, and an OCR process will glean most information for processing, including the supplier's company code and country. You will create a decision table that holds country codes and their corresponding continent (see Figure 7.8). The processing centers are simply named by the continent name. This decision table will only need to be maintained when the processing centers add or remove countries.

In keeping with your effort to not have to maintain responsibilities or some other table, all AP processors maintain their own parameter ID (PID) via transaction SU3, which is associated with their SAP user ID. This PID value will contain their AP processing center (see Figure 7.9).

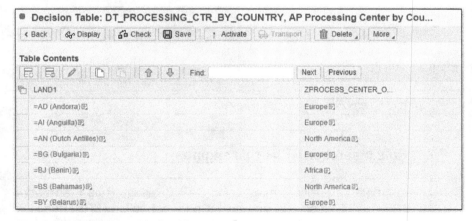

Figure 7.8: Decision table for AP processing center

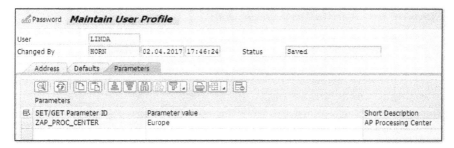

Figure 7.9: PID ZAP_PROC_CENTER set to Europe

Figure 7.10 shows all AP processors and their corresponding AP processing center PID assignments. Figure 7.11 shows that you have defined the possible agents of the AP processing task within the workflow definition as users of both AP processing roles ZSAP_FI_AP_INVOICE _PROC_ABC and ZSAP_FI_AP_INVOICE_PROC_XYZ representing business units ABC and XYZ. Figure 7.12 shows the intersection of AP role assignments and the AP processing center PIDs.

User Name	SET/GET Parameter ID	Parameter value
ANABELLA	ZAP_PROC_CENTER	Asia
DANIEL	ZAP_PROC_CENTER	
GLENDA	ZAP_PROC_CENTER	
TONY	ZAP_PROC_CENTER	
GARY	ZAP_PROC_CENTER	Europe
JOHN	ZAP_PROC_CENTER	
LINDA	ZAP_PROC_CENTER	
ALEX	ZAP_PROC_CENTER	North America
BRENDA	ZAP_PROC_CENTER	
GEORGE	ZAP_PROC_CENTER	
JENNIFER	ZAP_PROC_CENTER	
TRACI	ZAP_PROC_CENTER	
BILL	ZAP_PROC_CENTER	South America
DON	ZAP_PROC_CENTER	
DONNA	ZAP_PROC_CENTER	
PRICILLA	ZAP_PROC_CENTER	

Figure 7.10: AP processor assignment to AP processing center

171

Standard task: Maintain Agent Assignment

Attributes... 🗐 🗐 ℹ️ Org. assignment 🌐 🖼️	
▾ 👤 AP Invoice Processing	TS 88700140
▾ 🌐 Entry of Accounts Payable Invoices	AG ZSAP_FI_AP_INVOICE_PROC_ABC
• 👤 ALEX	US ALEX
• 👤 ANABELLA	US ANABELLA
• 👤 DANIEL	US DANIEL
• 👤 DON	US DON
• 👤 DONNA	US DONNA
• 👤 GEORGE	US GEORGE
• 👤 JENNIFER	US JENNIFER
• 👤 JOHN	US JOHN
• 👤 LINDA	US LINDA
• 👤 TONY	US TONY
▾ 🌐 Entry of Accounts Payable Invoices	AG ZSAP_FI_AP_INVOICE_PROC_XYZ
• 👤 BILL	US BILL
• 👤 BRENDA	US BRENDA
• 👤 GARY	US GARY
• 👤 GLENDA	US GLENDA
• 👤 PRICILLA	US PRICILLA
• 👤 TRACI	US TRACI

Figure 7.11: Definition of possible agents for AP processing task

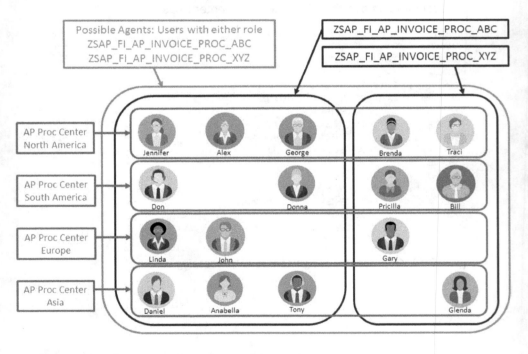

Figure 7.12: Business units and processing centers

7.2.2 BRF+ application

Now build an application that will determine the appropriate AP processors for the workflow task. Begin with an outline of what the BRF+ application will look like (see Listing 7.1). Figure 7.16 shows the four main roles as described in this listing.

BRF+ Application ZWFRULE

Function FN_WF_RULE

⇨ **Calls Ruleset RS_WF_RULE**

- **Rule 1** Decision Tree—Get role associated with the invoice's company code

- **Rule 2** Database Lookup—Get users assigned to the company code's role

- **Rule 3** Decision Table—Get AP processing center for invoice's country

- **Rule 4** Loop through users in company code's role

  ⇨ **Loop Rule 1: Read users' PIDs**

  - **Step 1—Initialize PID table**

  - **Step 2**—Procedure Call—Call BAPI to get a table of users' PIDs

  - **Step 3**—Loop through Users' PIDs

    → Find Users' AP Processing Center PIDs

  ⇨ **Loop Rule 2: Build responsible agents**

  - **Step 1**—If a user's AP Processing center PID value matches the invoice's processing center, add this user to the responsible agent table

Listing 7.1: Outline of BRF+ application

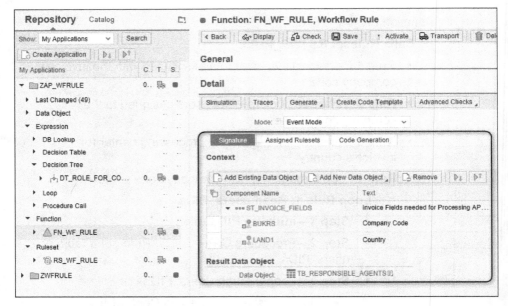

Figure 7.13: Function signature

Function FN_WF_RULE

Begin by defining the BRF+ application with the definition of a function. This function is the piece of the BRF+ application that interacts via a function module with the workflow rule.

The signature of the BRF+ function is comprised of a structure that holds the metadata from the invoice required for resolving the rule. In this case, you will need the company code to determine if the invoice is for business unit ABC or XYZ. You will also need to know the supplier's country, which is used to route the invoice to the appropriate processing center. In addition, the signature of your BRF+ function includes the result which will be a table of SAP agents. See Figure 7.13 for the function's signature.

This function is defined using EVENT MODE and there will be one assigned ruleset, meaning that priorities will not come into play, see Figure 7.14. Click on ASSIGNED RULESETS and then click on CREATE RULESET.

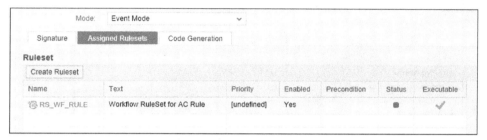

Figure 7.14: Function ruleset assignment

Ruleset RS_WF_RULE

To define the ruleset, drill into it from the function. The ruleset can be considered the conductor of the BRF+ application. Your ruleset calls multiple rules to obtain the result for the calling function. It reads a decision tree to determine which role to read for the agents. It calls a database lookup rule to read the agents assigned to that role. It reads the country-to-continent decision table to determine the correct AP processing center. It then calls a loop rule that will loop through each user to see if the user is assigned to the invoice's AP processing center; if they are, the user will be added to the table of responsible agents.

Because the ruleset has the same context as its calling function, you have all the variables contained in the calling function's context available, however, there are many variables needed that do not exist in the function's context. These will hold values that are needed between the rules, but not necessary to send back to the calling function. You will create these variables inside the ruleset as ruleset variables (see Figure 7.15). This is found in the detail section. You will need to toggle to DISPLAY RULESET HEADER if it is hidden.

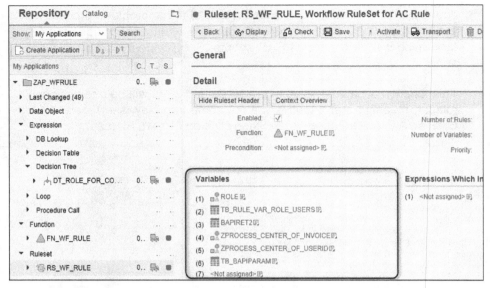

Figure 7.15: Ruleset variables

See Figure 7.16, for a ruleset that contains four rules.

Rule 1—Determine a role based on an invoice's company code

Defining the possible agents for the AP processing task is shown in Figure 7.11. You used two roles, one representing each of the two business units, ABC and XYZ. Now, consider runtime, when you will have an invoice. You want to filter out the processors who belong to the role associated with the invoice's company code from the possible agents.

Set up a decision tree, as shown in Figure 7.17, which will determine the role associated with the invoice's company code. This decision tree will return the appropriate role, which will be used by a subsequent rule in the ruleset to find the AP processors assigned to it. You can see from the decision tree that if the invoice's company code is 1000, the decision table will return the role associated with the XYZ business unit. If the invoice's company code does not equal 1000, processing will continue to the **x** value and the invoice's company code will be compared to 2000. If the invoice's company code is 2000, the decision tree will return the role belonging to the ABC business unit. If the invoice has any other company code, processing will continue to the next ✖ and will return role ZSAP_FI_AP_INVOICE_PROC_DEF, which would not be processed by this workflow. This decision tree is as basic as they come. Decision trees can hold hundreds of lines forking into multiple directions. Instead of being complicated, they provide a very organized way of presenting if/then logic.

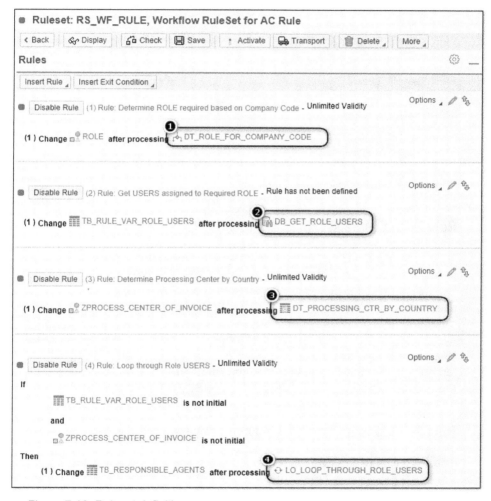

Figure 7.16: Ruleset definition

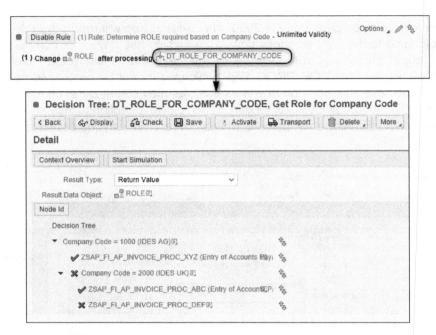

Figure 7.17: Ruleset rule 1, decision tree

Rule 2—Get users assigned to a role

Now that you have the role associated with the invoice, perform a database lookup to find the users assigned to this role. Note: Database lookups should be avoided, and instead, you should use an API, but to illustrate as many different rule types that can be built, for now, use a database lookup expression. Notice how you can take advantage of system variables in the select statement, e.g. system date can be used to ensure a role assignment is valid for the current date. From the selected records, the one field that is mapped, UNAME, will be loaded into the ruleset table TB_RULE_VAR_ROLE_USERS (see Figure 7.18).

Rule 3—Determine a processing center by the country

The third rule of the ruleset, as shown in Figure 7.19, will find the appropriate AP processing center based on the country of the invoice's supplier. For example, an invoice from a supplier based in Texas, in the United

States, will be routed to processors in the North America AP processing center.

Figure 7.18: Ruleset rule 2, database lookup expression

Rule 4—Loop through role users

The fourth and final rule of the ruleset, as shown in Figure 7.20 is the first rule with a precondition. The precondition makes sure that there is at least one user assigned to the role that corresponds to the invoice's company code. It also makes sure that an AP processing center was identified for the invoice. If both conditions are true, the rule will process a loop expression with mode, FOR EACH ENTRY IN..., table TB_RULE_VAR_ROLE_USERS. If the precondition fails, the ruleset will end processing and will return without having found any agents.

This loop expression in rule four, in turn, calls two of its own rules that will be processed for each row iteration. (See Listing 7.1 for a recap on the structure of the BRF+ application.) The first rule in the loop is the first rule that has multiple steps. The first step simply initializes the table that is populated with each user's parameter IDs. The second step, as shown in Figure 7.21, will perform a procedure call expression to obtain each user's parameter ID (PID) assignments.

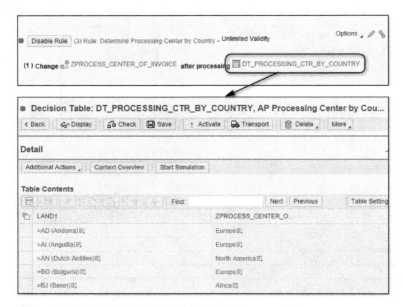

Figure 7.19: Ruleset rule 3, decision table expression

Default agent if no agent found

 Make sure that your workflow rule will respond in an appropriate manner if no agents are returned from the BRF+ application. You may decide to have an error issued in the workflow when there are no agents. This will trigger an email to the global workflow administrator or to a workflow-specific administrator if one is defined for the workflow definition. The workflow administrator will then be able to correct the agent issue and re-trigger the agent rule. Alternatively, you could add an additional rule to your BRF+ ruleset that will assign a default agent if no other agents have been found.

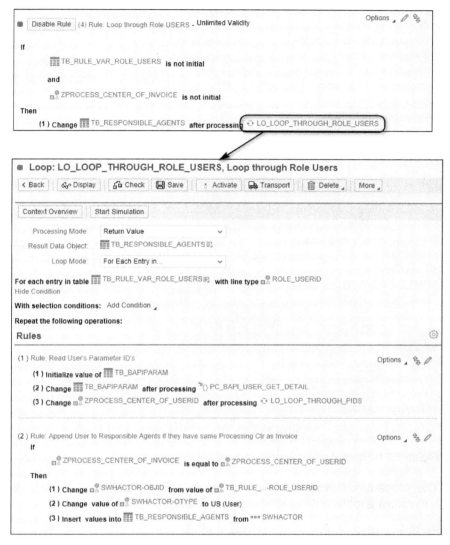

Figure 7.20: Ruleset rule 4, loop expression

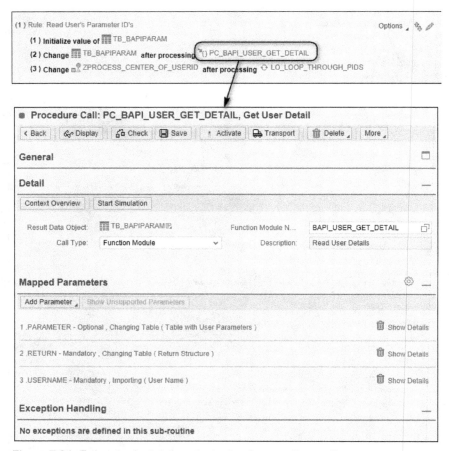

Figure 7.21: Ruleset rule 4, loop rule 1, step 2, procedure call

The procedure call will call function module BAPI_USER_GET_DETAIL and return a table holding all the users' PIDs.

Once the PIDs are obtained in step two, the third step of the first rule of the loop, as shown in Figure 7.22, will process another loop to find the only PID you are interested in, ZAP_PROC_CENTER. This loop is like the other loop in that it is processed using mode, FOR EACH ENTRY IN..., table TB_BAPIPARAM. The difference here is that there is a selection condition; your loop will only process a record from the table if it meets the criteria of the parameter ID being equal to the one you are looking for, PARID = "ZAP_PROC_CENTER". If this PID is found, the value associated with the PID is collected. This value holds the processing center of the AP processor.

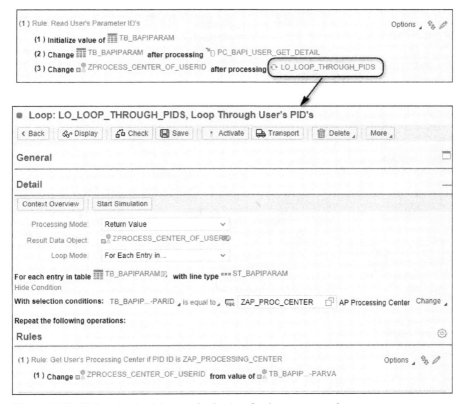

Figure 7.22: Ruleset rule 4, loop rule 1, step 3—loop expression

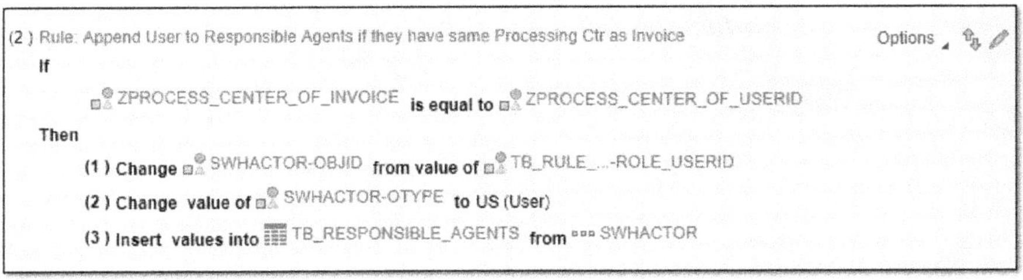

Figure 7.23: Ruleset rule 4, loop rule 2

The second rule of this loop rule, which is step 4 of the main ruleset, as shown in Figure 7.23, is where you compare the processing center of the AP processor with the invoice's processing center. If they are the same, the AP processor will be added to the list of agents who will be returned by the ruleset to the BRF+ function.

That completes the construction of the BRF+ application. Now take advantage of BRF+'s testing tools. Go back to the function FN_WF_RULE and click on the SIMULATION button, see Figure 7.24. Click CONTINUE on the subsequent screen and it will take you to the simulation tool (see Figure 7.25).

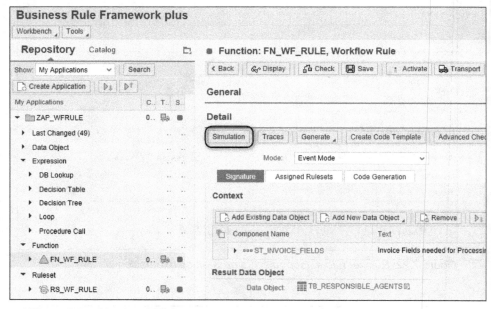

Figure 7.24: Simulate function button for a function

Figure 7.25: Simple simulation example

In Figure 7.25, the structure of the function's context is populated with 1000 for the invoice's company code (BUKRS) and US for the invoice's country (LAND1). You know from the decision tree, Rule 1 of the ruleset, role ZSAP_FI_AP_INVOICE_PROC_XYZ is assigned for company code 1000 (see Figure 7.17). You know from the decision table, Rule 3 of the ruleset, the AP processing center for the United States is North America (see Figure 7.19). Now refer to Figure 7.12 to see the rule returned the correct processors, Brenda and Traci.

If you click on the ⌗ Execute and Display Processing Steps button that is to the right of the EXECUTE button as shown in Figure 7.25, you will receive an incredibly detailed account of everything that happens.

185

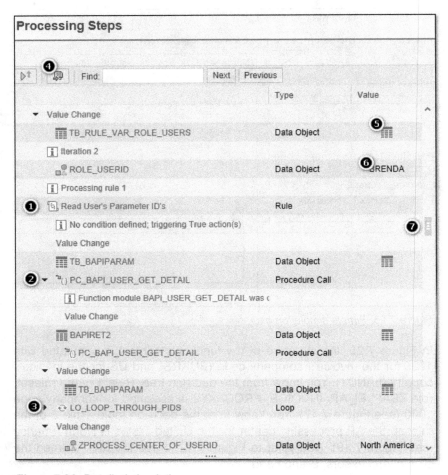

Figure 7.26: Detailed simulation

Compare Figure 7.26 to the outline in Listing 7.1 and you will see how the outline is followed. You can click on the TABLE icons in Figure 7.26 to see all the entries in the tables. BRF+ is very easy to debug because of its extraordinary simulation tools.

Figure 7.26 is a snippet of the detailed simulation. If you look at Listing 7.1, you can see that the portion of the simulation is Rule 4.

❶, ❷, and ❸ show where an expression is being called; notice the grey lines they appear on.

❹ This entire simulation can be downloaded to MS Excel.

The lighter-colored lines in Figure 7.26 show data objects. ❺ Table TB_RULE_VAR_ROLE_USERS can be double-clicked to see the table entries. ❻ Variable ROLE_USERID shows the value BRENDA.

❼ shows the scroll bar; this lets you know that the view is a very small subset of all the processing steps.

Figure 7.27: BRF+ will generate function module or Web service

7.2.3   Workflow rule

Before creating a workflow rule, create the function module that the rule will call. The BRF+ rule engine helps by creating a code template (see Figure 7.28). Alternatively, BRF+ can build a complete Web service or function module (see Figure 7.27). Decide to have code generated in a template and then insert this code into the function module that has the required signature for a workflow rule.

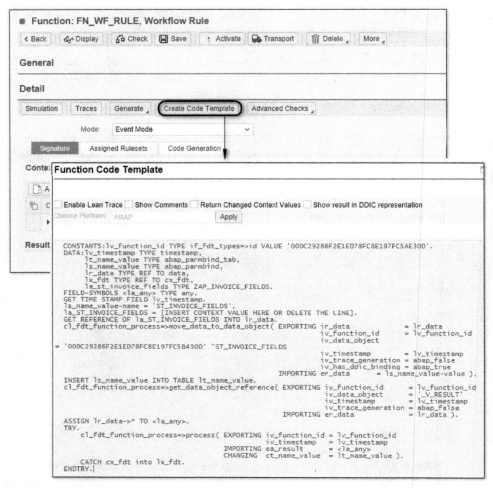

Figure 7.28: Generate code template from BRF+ function

The function module will retrieve the 'BUKRS' and 'LAND1' values from the rule container, which is bound to the workflow container. It will then make a call to the BRF+ function to retrieve the agents based on the container values. Once it has received the agents, it will load them into the ACTOR_TAB table for the rule. Listing 7.2 shows the function module that will be used in the workflow rule. It has the required signature and you have inserted the code that was generated from BRF+.

```
FUNCTION z_ap_inv_proc_wf_rule_brf .
*"----------------------------------------------------------------
*"*"Local Interface:
*"  TABLES
*"      ACTOR_TAB STRUCTURE  SWHACTOR
*"      AC_CONTAINER STRUCTURE  SWCONT
*"  EXCEPTIONS
*"      NOBODY_FOUND
*"----------------------------------------------------------------
  INCLUDE <cntain>. ❶

  CONSTANTS:
    lc_brf_struc    TYPE ifw_de_comm_structure_name
                    VALUE 'ST_INVOICE_FIELDS',
    lc_function_id  TYPE ifw_de_function_id
                    VALUE '000C29286F2E1ED78FC8E197FC5AE30D',
    lc_brf_struc_id TYPE sysuuid_c
                    VALUE '000C29286F2E1ED78FC8E197FC5B430D'.

  DATA: ls_inv_fields      TYPE zap_invoice_fields,
        ls_name_value      TYPE abap_parmbind,
        lt_name_value      TYPE abap_parmbind_tab,
        ls_actor_tab       TYPE swhactor,
        lv_timestamp       TYPE timestamp,
        lr_data            TYPE REF TO data,
        lr_invoice_fields  TYPE REF TO data.

  FIELD-SYMBOLS:
    <fs_any>              TYPE ANY TABLE,
    <fs_actor>            TYPE any,
    <lr_invoice_fields> TYPE any.

  REFRESH: actor_tab.
  CLEAR: ls_inv_fields, ls_name_value, lt_name_value.
  GET TIME STAMP FIELD lv_timestamp.

* Get Values from Rule Container ❷
  swc_get_element ac_container 'BUKRS' ls_inv_fields-bukrs.
  swc_get_element ac_container 'LAND1' ls_inv_fields-land1.
```

```
    IF ls_inv_fields-bukrs IS INITIAL.
      RAISE nobody_found. ❸
    ENDIF.

    TRY.
*       Assign Rule Container values to BRF+ objects
        ls_name_value-name = lc_brf_struc.
        CREATE DATA lr_invoice_fields TYPE zap_invoice_fields.
        ASSIGN lr_invoice_fields->* TO <lr_invoice_fields>.
        <lr_invoice_fields> = ls_inv_fields.
        lr_data = lr_invoice_fields.
    ❹   cl_fdt_function_process=>move_data_to_data_object(
            EXPORTING ir_data             = lr_data
                      iv_function_id      = lc_function_id
                      iv_data_object      = lc_brf_struc_id
                      iv_timestamp        = lv_timestamp
                      iv_trace_generation = abap_false
                      iv_has_ddic_binding = abap_false
            IMPORTING er_data             = ls_name_value-value ).
        INSERT ls_name_value INTO TABLE lt_name_value.

    ❺   cl_fdt_function_process=>get_data_object_reference(
            EXPORTING iv_function_id      = lc_function_id
                      iv_data_object      = '_V_RESULT'
                      iv_timestamp        = lv_timestamp
                      iv_trace_generation = abap_false
            IMPORTING er_data             = lr_data ).

        ASSIGN lr_data->* TO <fs_any>.

*       Call BRF+ Function
    ❻   cl_fdt_function_process=>process(
            EXPORTING iv_function_id = lc_function_id
                      iv_timestamp   = lv_timestamp
            IMPORTING ea_result      = <fs_any>
            CHANGING  ct_name_value  = lt_name_value ).
      CATCH cx_fdt.
    ENDTRY.
```

```
LOOP AT <fs_any> ASSIGNING <fs_actor>. ❼
  MOVE-CORRESPONDING <fs_actor> TO ls_actor_tab.
  APPEND ls_actor_tab TO actor_tab.
ENDLOOP.

ENDFUNCTION.
```

Listing 7.2: Workflow rule function module

❶ INCLUDE <cntain> contains macros that read the rule container which is passed in as an import parameter.

❷ BUKRS, the company code and LAND1, the country of the invoice, are retrieved from the container, ac_container, which is a table passed into the function module. These values are written to structure ls_inv_fields.

❸ If no company code is found in the container, the exception, noboby_found will be raised and will cause the workflow instance to go into error status. This is because the rule is set to terminate if the function module does not find any agents.

❹ Method cl_fdt_function_process=>move_data_to_data_object is called to package the container elements in a way that the BRF+ process method requires. The structure LS_NAME_VALUE, as shown in Figure 7.29, is returned and loaded into LT_NAME_VALUE, which represents the rule container for BRF+.

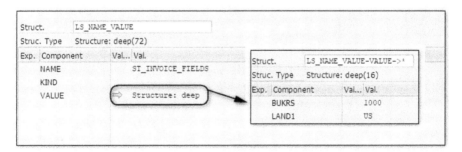

Figure 7.29: Structure LS_NAME_VALUE

❺ Method cl_fdt_function_process=>get_data_object_reference is called to read the result type from the function you will be calling. The result type will be a table of a two-field structure that will hold the agents (OTYPE + OBJID).

❻ Method cl_fdt_function_process=>process is where the actual call to the BRF+ function is made. The container elements are passed to the function in the table LT_NAME_VALUE and the agents are returned in the field symbol <FS_ANY>.

❼ The agents returned from the BRF+ function call are copied to the table in the function module that holds the agents found.

Now that you have completed the function module, you are finally ready to build the workflow rule (see Figure 7.31). Go to transaction PFAC to build it. Name the rule and change the category to AGENT DETERMINATION: FUNCTION TO BE EXECUTED and enter the function module name, Z_AP_INV_PROC_WF_RULE_BRF. Click on the CONTAINER tab and enter the container elements (see Figure 7.30).

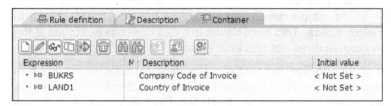

Figure 7.30: Rule container elements

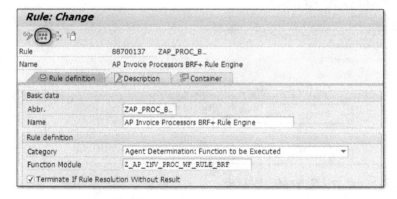

Figure 7.31: Workflow rule

192

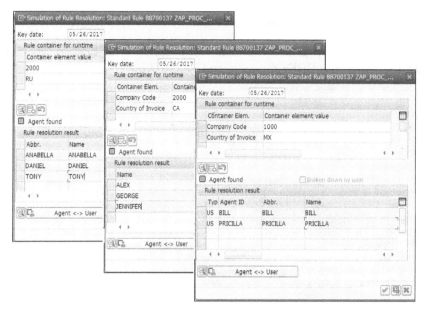

Figure 7.32: Simulating the rule

Click on the SIMULATE icon ⬚ from inside t-code PFAC, as shown in Figure 7.31, to test the rule. Load values for the rule container elements, as shown in Figure 7.32, and compare results to AP processing agents as defined in Figure 7.12.

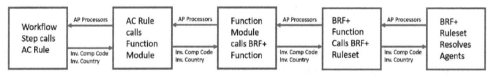

Figure 7.33: Workflow rule to call BRF+ ruleset

Figure 7.33 depicts the data flow from the workflow step with the rule to the BRF+ ruleset to obtain the agents and then the flow of how the agents are returned to the workflow.

Create a task that automatically calls a BRF+ function

An alternative way to use the BRF+ application is to build a workflow task that calls your BRF+ function, see Figure 7.34.

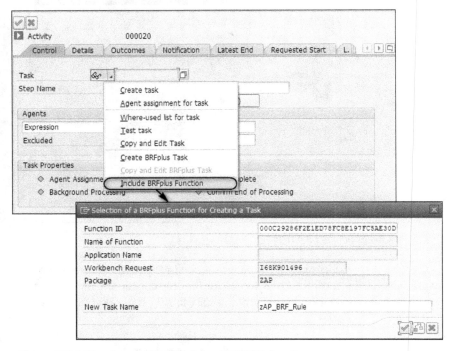

Figure 7.34: Create workflow task to call BRF+ function

Notice THE WORKBENCH REQUEST and the PACKAGE default in from the workflow. These must match the workbench request and package of the BRF+ application. Hitting the [Enter] key will auto-populate the function name and the application name, as shown in Figure 7.35. Clicking on the GREEN CHECK MARK will create the task. A pop-up to store the new task in a transport is populated and then and you will be presented with the automated binding.

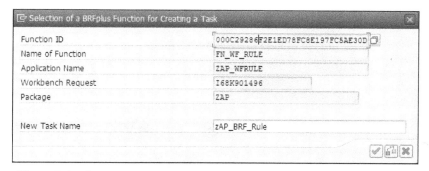

Figure 7.35: Function name and application name auto-populate

Figure 7.36 shows the workflow step calling the new task that was created.

❶ Binding from workflow container to BRF+ task is shown.

❷ The workflow engine recognizes the task as a BRF+ task and provides an icon that can be clicked to go to the BRF+ application.

This function will expect the task container to hold the input parameter values for the BRF+ function and will return an expression that will be used to hold the agents. See Figure 7.13 for the BRF+ function's signature. The BRF+ task calls the method EXECUTE of an automatically generated class (see Figure 7.36).

I prefer creating a rule as opposed to this alternative way of creating a task that calls the function for three reasons:

1. The workflow definition will have fewer steps.

2. A background process is not required when processing a rule as it is when a background task calls the BRF+ function.

3. No error can be triggered, as it can be from the rule, if there are no agents found.

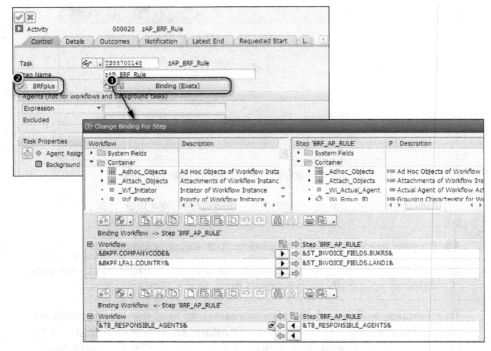

Figure 7.36: Workflow step showing generated BRF task

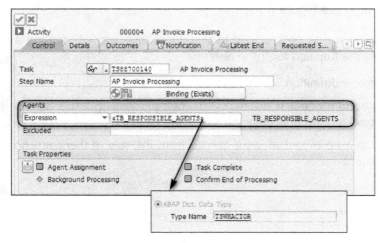

Figure 7.37: Expression is used for agents

Figure 7.37 shows how the expression, TB_RESPONSIBLE_AGENTS, which is created from a background task, as shown in Figure 7.38, is used to assign agents to the AP invoice processing step.

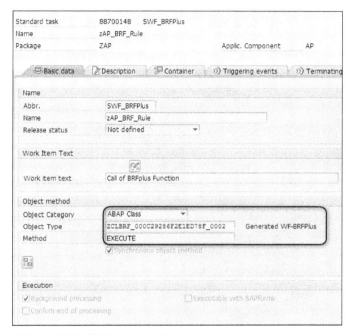

Figure 7.38: BRF generated task

7.3 Modeled deadline—escalation

Section 1.4 discussed escalation agents. Now consider notifying escalation agents and changing the workflow direction because a step went into deadline status. This means that the escalation agent can now take over processing, depending on how the escalation step is defined. Consider the following example. You have a workflow that currently sends a reminder to the original agent(s) for the invoice approval work step. The reminder is sent five days after the work item is created if it has not yet been completed. Unfortunately, the reminders are being ignored and the invoices are not being approved on time.

You decide to convert the reminder into an escalation step. Instead of sending a reminder to the invoice approver, now an actual invoice approval work item will be sent to the original approver's superior. The escalation agent can now process the work item so that follow-on steps can be processed. You decide to leave the original approval work item ready in the invoice approver's SAP Business Workplace inbox; this will allow the approval to be performed by either the original approver or the approver's superior. Once either approval happens, the approval work item that was not executed will be cancelled, either automatically or by a process control step.

The first activity to transform the reminder to an escalation work item to be sent to the superior is to change the LATEST END action from DISPLAY TEXT, as shown in Figure 7.39, to MODELED, as shown in Figure 7.40. Then add a description to LATEST END DEADLINE OCCURRED for the outcome.

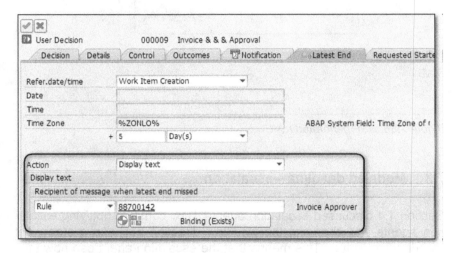

Figure 7.39: Latest end deadline action is set to DISPLAY TEXT

Simple example

 To keep the example simple, there are no processing steps defined subsequent to either the approval or rejection actions. In a real-life workflow definition, there would be additional steps under these paths. By not adding processing steps, you can focus on the workflow direction.

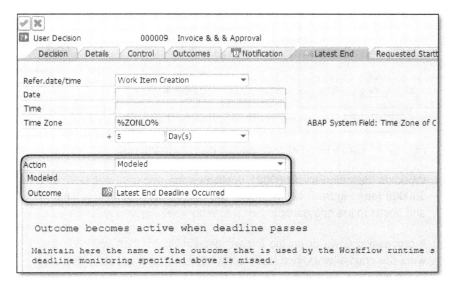

Figure 7.40: Latest end deadline action changed to MODELED

By changing the action of the latest end reminder to MODELED, the workflow definition will change, as shown in Figure 7.41. The second image shows a new outcome that ends with the outcome label you added, LATEST END DEADLINE OCCURRED. This new path does not lead to the workflow completed end. If processing goes down the escalation path, you will use a process control step to get control back to the main processing path. A process control step will allow you to manipulate the processing of the workflow instance.

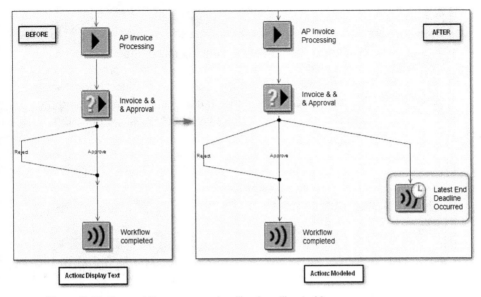

Figure 7.41: Convert DISPLAY TEXT deadline handling to MODELED

Workflow definition step 000021 duplicates the approval decision, step 000009 (see Figure 7.42), however, the rule for step 000021 is different and points to the original approver's superior (see Figure 7.43).

If processing flows down the missed deadline path, then you no longer want the original work item to be completed. Add a process control step to the workflow definition to set the original approval step to be obsolete. Before you can set the original work item to obsolete, you must provide an outcome on the step for this processing path.

Go to workflow step 000009 and on the OUTCOMES tab, activate the outcome, PROCESSING OBSOLETE. This is a standard outcome that is always available and is created in a disabled state. See Figure 7.44 to see where this outcome is disabled and Figure 7.45 to see where it has been enabled.

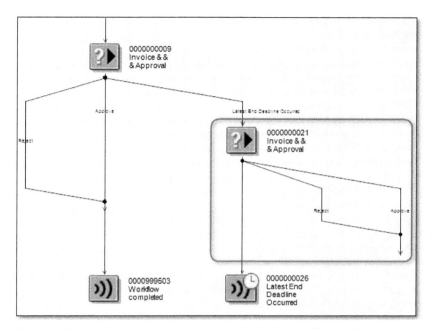

Figure 7.42: Duplicated approval step is added it to deadline path

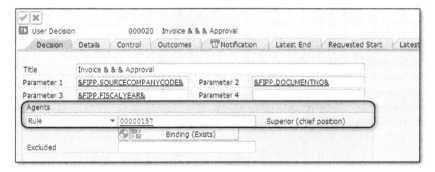

Figure 7.43: Add the rule for an agent's superior to the escalation step

201

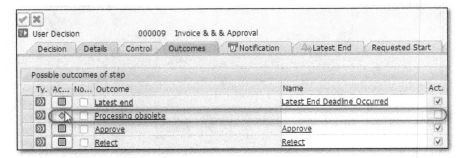

Figure 7.44: Outcome processing obsolete is disabled

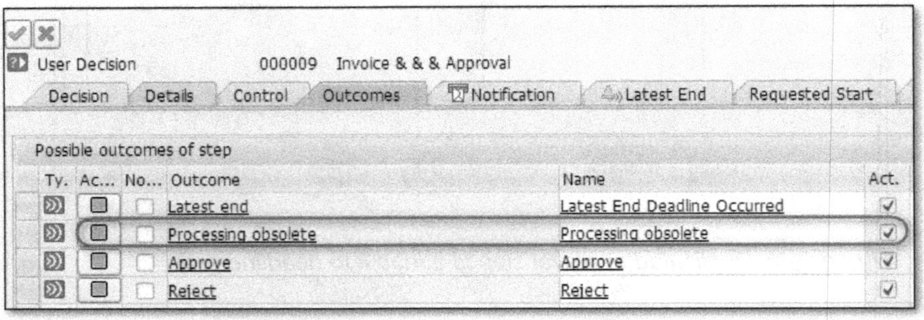

Figure 7.45: Outcome PROCESSING OBSOLETE toggled to ENABLED

By toggling this outcome on, you will have a new path proceeding from the original approval step, labeled, PROCESSING OBSOLETE as shown by ❶ in Figure 7.46 This path allows the task to be completed without going down either the approval or rejection path, which, in a real-world scenario would have processing steps. If escalation occurs, you do not want to process approval or rejection steps because they will be processed after the new escalation step.

Now add the process control step. The process control step will be added in the workflow definition after the new approval step's outcome of APPROVE or REJECT. After either an invoice approval or rejection from the superior, you will need to set the original approval work item to obsolete. You do this with a process control step. See ❷ in Figure 7.46, for where to single click to select and then click on ⬚ and select PROCESS CONTROL. There are many process control options. Select SET WORK ITEM TO

OBSOLETE from the options available, as shown in Figure 7.47. You can see the resulting step indicated in Figure 7.49.

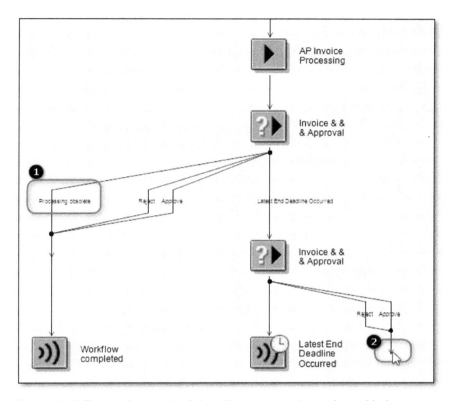

Figure 7.46: Processing an obsolete path once an outcome is enabled

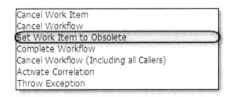

Figure 7.47: Process control processing options

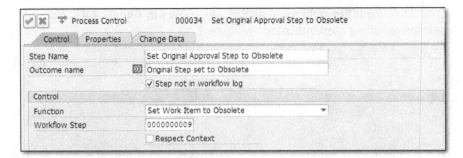

Figure 7.48: Process control cancelling workflow step 000009

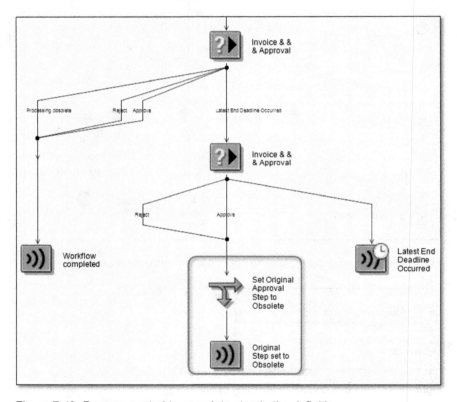

Figure 7.49: Process control to complete step in the definition

The graphical log, shown in Figure 7.50, shows a workflow instance where the original approval work item ❶ is sent to the original invoice approver, but is not processed before the work item goes into latest-end deadline status, ❷. The superior of the original invoice approver approves the invoice ❸. The approval of this second work item leads the process flow to ❹, the process control step. When you defined the process control step, as shown in Figure 7.48, you were able to select which step to set to obsolete; step 000009. The process control step will set the original approval work item ❶ to obsolete, which leads the workflow processing down the PROCESSING OBSOLETE path, which leads to WORK-FLOW COMPLETED.

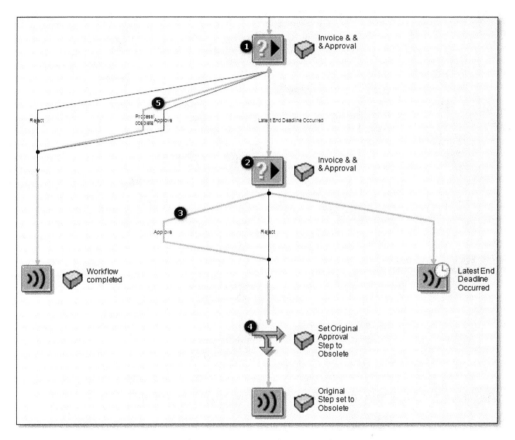

Figure 7.50: Graphical workflow log, approval by superior

Alternatively, another workflow instance of the same workflow definition may complete from the original approval work item even after the escalation approval work item was created. Figure 7.51 shows a graphical

205

workflow log where the original approval work item went into LATEST END DEADLINE status and an approval work item was sent to the original approver's superior. However, the original approver approves the invoice before his superior could. Because processing was completed down the approval path of the original approval work item, as shown in Figure 7.51 by ❸, the escalation approval work item is automatically set to LOGICALLY DELETED, as shown in Figure 7.51 by ❹. No process control step is necessary if logic flows from the original approval work item.

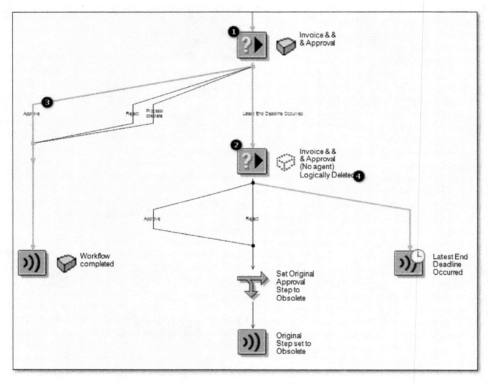

Figure 7.51: Graphical workflow log, approval by original agent

7.4 Ad hoc agent selection

Sometimes the only way the proper agent for your workflow process can be determined is when there is human intervention. This is when you use ad hoc agent selection. Keep in mind, there should still be constraints as to which agents are possible for selection.

7.4.1 Ad hoc agent selection at start of workflow

A prime use of ad hoc agent selection is when a user starts a workflow from a transaction via GOS and wants to designate the agent(s). The ad hoc selection will happen before the workflow begins. The user who starts the workflow will select the agent(s) to perform the dialog task(s) in the workflow that have the ad hoc container element as their task agent assignment. The agent starting the workflow can choose from a list of agents who are the possible agents of tasks the selected agent(s) will perform.

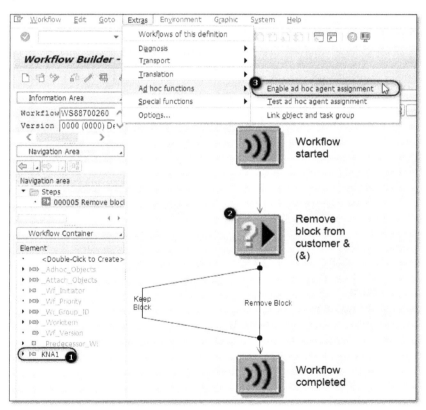

Figure 7.52: Enable ad hoc agent assignment wizard

SAP provides a wizard that will create a workflow container element that will hold the ad hoc agent(s) selected at run time. This container element will be automatically assigned to the task that is selected to be the task that the ad hoc agent(s) will perform.

Before initiating the ad hoc agent wizard, set up a new workflow definition. Build a workflow that can be started by someone via GOS directly from a transaction that supports the KNA1 business object. To have the workflow available to start from a customer transaction, you must put the business object, KNA1, in the workflow container (see ❶ in Figure 7.52). The container element is defined as an import parameter. Next, create the first workflow step, which will be a decision step (see ❷ in Figure 7.52). This will be the step that the ad hoc agent(s) perform. Note: In Figure 7.53, when defining the step, you do not include the task agent.

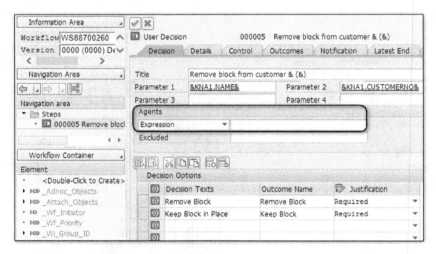

Figure 7.53: Workflow step that will be modified by ad hoc wizard

Once you have created the step to be executed by the ad hoc agent(s), initiate the ad hoc agent wizard. Click on EXTRAS ⇨ AD HOC FUNCTIONS ⇨ ENABLE AD HOC AGENT ASSIGNMENT (see ❸ in Figure 7.52). The first screen of the wizard provides information (see Figure 7.54).

208

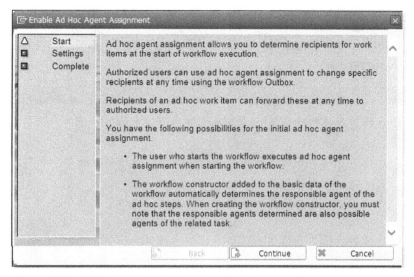

Figure 7.54: Ad hoc agent assignment wizard screen 1

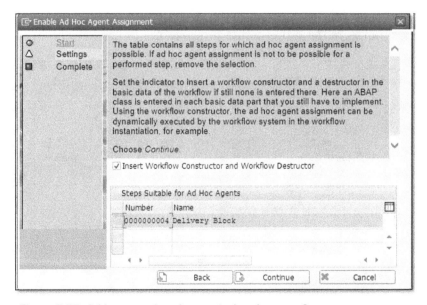

Figure 7.55: Ad hoc agent assignment wizard screen 2

The second screen, as shown in Figure 7.55 shows all the steps with missing agents. Select the step and click CONTINUE. You are taken to another information screen, as shown in Figure 7.56. Read it and then click COMPLETE.

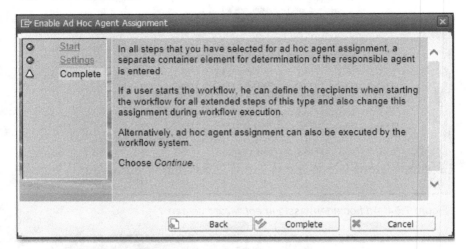

Figure 7.56: Ad hoc agent assignment wizard screen 3

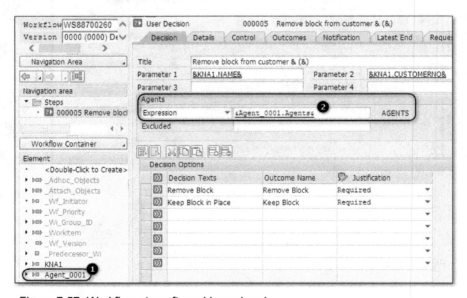

Figure 7.57: Workflow step after ad hoc wizard

210

Once the wizard is completed, you can see the changes that were made to the workflow definition. Figure 7.57 ❶ shows the new workflow container element, Agent_0001. This container element is an import parameter with business object AAGENT. The wizard sets the step agent of the task you selected as a multiline attribute of this business object (see Figure 7.57 ❷).

You need to do one more thing to the workflow that will allow users to start the workflow from GOS within customer transactions. As mentioned earlier, by putting the business object KNA1 in the workflow container, this workflow is available in customer transactions when the user clicks on the GOS icon and then selects START WORKFLOW, as seen in Figure 7.59. However, before the workflow starts, the user needs to provide the possible agents who will be able to start this workflow. To do this, the user will click on FIND AGENTS…, as seen in Figure 7.60.

Figure 7.58 shows where you have assigned a customer maintenance role to this workflow. This list shows the only agents who have the workflow available to start from GOS. They will see the workflow in their list, as seen in the left panel of Figure 7.60. Users who do not have this role will not see the workflow in their list of available workflows.

Figure 7.58: Assign agents to workflow task

211

Select ad hoc agents and start the workflow

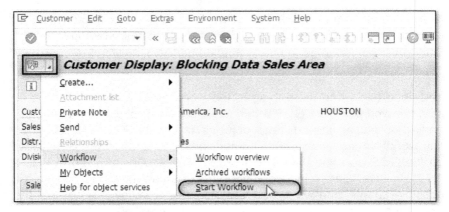

Figure 7.59: From GOS menu, select START WORKFLOW

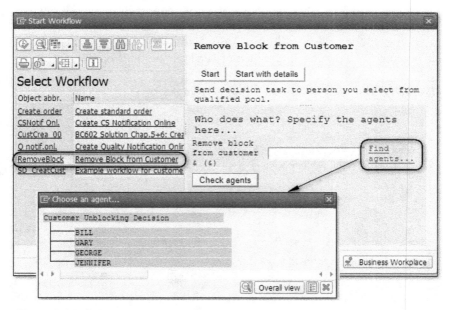

Figure 7.60: Select ad hoc agent from agent list

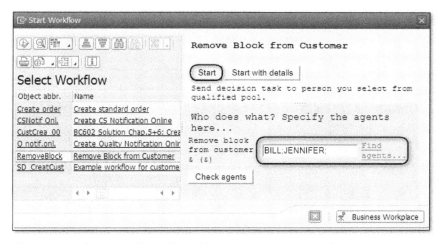

Figure 7.61: Start workflow after ad hoc agents are selected

You may select multiple ad hoc agents simply by clicking on FIND AGENTS and selecting an agent, then clicking on FIND AGENTS again and selecting another agent. If you want to add agents manually, keep the names separated by colons, see Figure 7.61. Once you click START, a workflow instance will begin. And finally, as shown in Figure 7.62, the selected ad hoc agents are indeed the agents of the task.

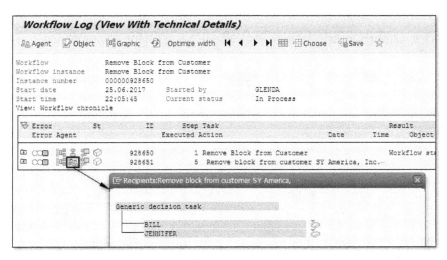

Figure 7.62: Workflow instance with agents of remove block task

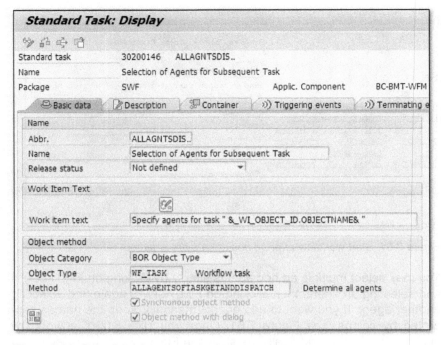

Figure 7.63: Selection of agents for subsequent task

7.4.2 Ad hoc agent selection as task of workflow

The example given in Section 7.4.1 requires user intervention to begin a workflow when a customer is blocked. What if you want to change this to allow the *event* of the customer being blocked to begin the workflow? The workflow will begin automatically, and the workflow initiator will determine the agent in an ad hoc manner for a subsequent step in the workflow.

SAP provides a standard task that can be used to allow an agent to choose the agent for a subsequent task in a workflow (see Figure 7.63). Figure 7.64 shows the agent assignment and the binding from the workflow to the task. ❶ shows where the agent is assigned as the workflow initiator. ❷ shows X sent as the value for the task element SELECT MULTIPLE which means that the workflow initiator can select multiple ad hoc agents.

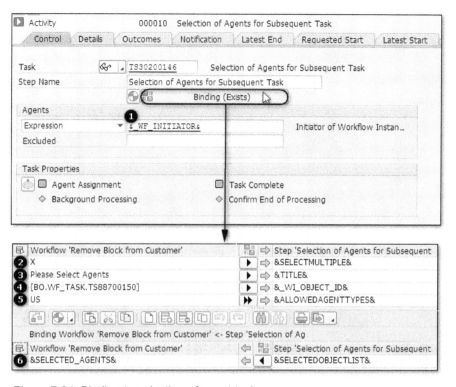

Figure 7.64: Binding to selection of agent task

The task allows a title to be given through the binding (see ❸). Task TS88700150 is instantiated and passed to task TS30200146 (see ❹). This task provides the list of agents who can be selected from for the ad hoc agent selection. Task TS30200146 will read the possible agents of the instantiated task passed to it and use these possible agents for the ad hoc selection list. ❺ is where you tell task TS30200146 what type of agents can be selected. In this example, you used US and only users will be presented for selection (see Figure 7.65). The task element ALLOWED AGENT TYPES can also be left unpopulated and all possible agent types will be presented for selection. ❻ shows the selected agents, which are returned as a table type HROBJEC_14. This table will be assigned as an expression to a subsequent step.

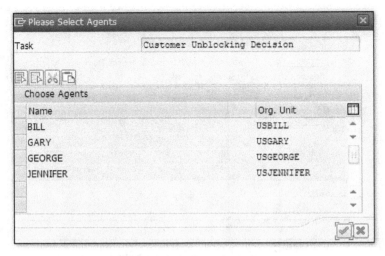

Figure 7.65: Pop-up for agents to be selected

Easy instantiation

 You can instantiate a business object in your binding by using the following format: [BO.BUS_OBJ.OBJ_KEY] e.g. to instantiate the task business object WF_TASK with task TS88700150 you would bind the following: [BO.WF_TASK.TS88700150] to the business object WF_TASK in the target task. Note: This trick only works with specific values; it does not work with variables.

7.5   Release procedure agents

SAP provides multiple workflow definitions that can be configured by an analyst with very limited workflow knowledge. One example is the release procedure functionality for multiple purchasing documents: the purchase requisition, contract, outline agreement, and purchase order.

For this workshop, you are going to look at the rule SAP provides for the requisition which will find agents based on configuration for the release codes. This rule will work for releases on the requisition based at the header level (BOR object BUS2009) or releases based at the item level (BOR BUS2015). The workshop example will be with the item-level release. The rule works in conjunction with configuration for release procedures using classification.

This workshop will show a very shallow dive into the class and characteristics definition to fulfil the classification configuration required to build very simple release procedures. There will be only two characteristics defined for the release procedure class. This workshop will mostly focus on the release codes that are ultimately assigned to the purchasing document line items by these release procedures.

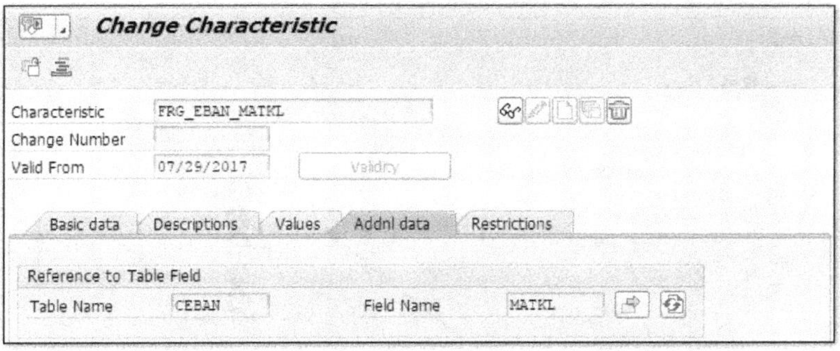

Figure 7.66: Characteristic definition

To get to the character definition area, go to MATERIALS MANAGEMENT • PURCHASING • PURCHASE REQUISITION • RELEASE PROCEDURE • PROCEDURE WITH CLASSIFICATION • EDIT CHARACTERISTIC.

Figure 7.66 shows one of two characteristics that will be used in this workshop. FRG_EBAN_MATKL will point to the material group field, MATKL. Notice the table reference for this field is a communication structure, CEBAN, and not the table EBAN. The other characteristic, FRG_EBAN_GSWRT points to field CEBAN-GSWRT.

217

Figure 7.67: Class definition

To edit classes, go to MATERIALS MANAGEMENT • PURCHASING • PURCHASE
REQUISITION • RELEASE PROCEDURE • PROCEDURE WITH CLASSIFICATION •
EDIT CLASSES.

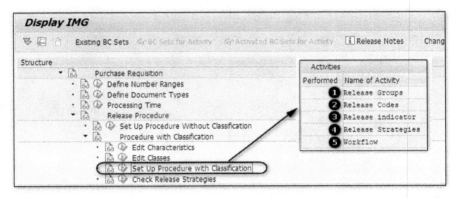

Figure 7.68: Purchase requisition release code configuration

To set up a classification procedure, go to MATERIALS MANAGEMENT •
PURCHASING • PURCHASE REQUISITION • RELEASE PROCEDURE • PROCE-
DURE WITH CLASSIFICATION • SET UP PROCEDURE WITH CLASSIFICATION.

Figure 7.67 shows the class, FRG_EBAN_BUS2105. The class name
includes the BOR object BUS2105, which is keyed at the requisition-item
level. This naming convention makes it obvious that the characteristics
assigned to this class can reference item-level fields, although the characteristics can also reference header fields. If there was a class named
FRG_EBAN_BUS2009, you would expect it to contain only characteristics referencing header-level fields.

Once the class has been created and has its characteristics assigned, release codes can be configured. Figure 7.68 shows where this configuration resides on the IMG.

❶ of Figure 7.68 shows where the release groups are defined. There is only one release group defined, 01 (see Figure 7.69). The release object of 1, which cannot be changed, refers to the purchasing document for the release code, which is the requisition. The column OVRELPREQ, short for "Overall Release for Purchase Requisition" is a checkbox, which if checked, means the release will be at the requisition's header level and the BOR object used is BUS2009. It is not checked, which means that the releases will be at the requisition item level and will use BOR object BUS2015. The class FRG_EBAN_BUS2105 is assigned to release group 01 and finally the release group description, PREQ REL GROUP is given.

Figure 7.69: Release group definition

Release groups based on OVRRELPREQ value

 Release groups will only be effective for document types that are also defined with the same value for field OVRRELPREQ. Because release group has the overall release flag turned off, this release group will only go into effect for document types with the same setting.

---

❷ of Figure 7.68 is where the release codes are defined. There are three release codes configured (see Figure 7.70). All three defined release codes belong to release group 01. Agents for the release procedure workflows are assigned based on the release codes. There are multiple ways agents can be assigned to the release codes. The WORKFLOW column is where choosing one of three possibilities for assigning agents is made. Blank means that the release code is not applicable for the workflow; these releases must be performed directly in a release transaction. Assigning a 1 means that the rule will read the workflow section of the release procedure configuration to assign agents. The final option is to assign the release code the value '9', which means the rule will obtain the agent using a custom code found in a user exit. This will be discussed in greater detail at the end of this workshop.

Rule design considerations

 If you are going to assign the '9' value to all the release codes, you might want to rethink whether to just create a new rule to use. If, for example, it would make more sense to use a rule with responsibilities instead of having to write ABAP in a user exit, you will want to change the setting for all your release codes to space instead of '9' and update your workflow to use your new rule. On the other hand, there is a lot to be said for visibility. Most analysts and developers, when it comes to release procedures, are used to looking in the IMG to find out how agents are assigned.

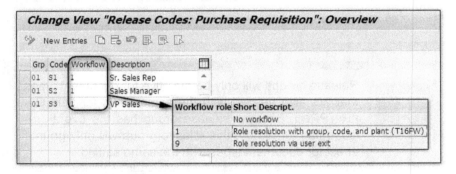

Figure 7.70: Release code agent assignment options

❸ of Figure 7.68 shows where the release indicators are defined. Release indicators direct the purchasing document on what is allowed based on release status. This basic example uses the two indicators that are circled, as shown in Figure 7.71. All purchasing documents that fall under release procedures have a release indicator. The purchase requisitions will initially have the indicator, BLOCKED, then when all releases have been affected, it will be changed to RFQ/PURCHASE ORDER. This means the purchase requisition can then be converted to an RFQ or to a purchase order.

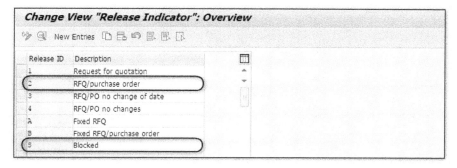

Figure 7.71: Release indicator definition

❹ of Figure 7.68 is where the release group, the release codes, and the release indicators all come together to define the release strategies. There are three release strategies defined for this example (see Figure 7.72).

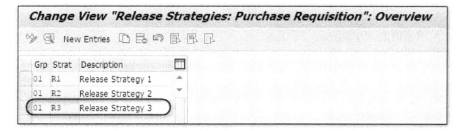

Figure 7.72: Release strategy definition

Take a closer look at strategy R3 to see how strategies are defined (see Figure 7.73). Each release strategy can have up to eight release levels (release codes) assigned. Release strategy R3 contains the three release groups you defined: S1, S2, and S3. Once the release codes have been listed, the prerequisites for each release code must be defined.

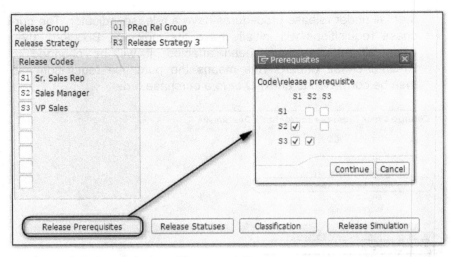

Figure 7.73: Release strategy R3 prerequisites

Figure 7.73 shows the release prerequisites for strategy R3. The release prerequisites determine which releases are required before other releases can be made. In the workshop example, the release codes must be released in a simple stair-step sequence. There is no prerequisite for release code S1. Release code S2 requires the release of S1 before it can be released. Release code S3 requires the release of code S2, which of course, requires the release of S1.

Once the prerequisites have been defined, the release statuses can be defined (see Figure 7.74). This is where the previously defined release indicators (see Figure 7.71) come into play. The columns for each release code show all possible release combinations. This grid is built based on the release prerequisites made and cannot be changed, unless, of course, you go back and change the prerequisites. What SAP wants you to do here is to define the release status for each release combination. Again, the example is as simple as it can get, the requisition will be blocked until all three releases have been given. If releases S1, S2, and S3 have been released, as indicated by the check marks in the columns, then it is possible for the requisition to be turned into an RFQ or a purchase order, otherwise, the requisition is blocked and cannot be used.

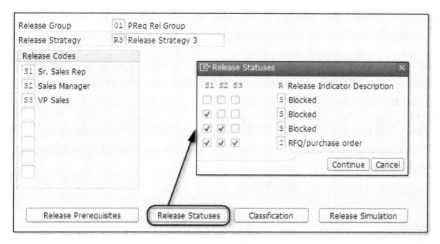

Figure 7.74: Release strategy R3 release statuses

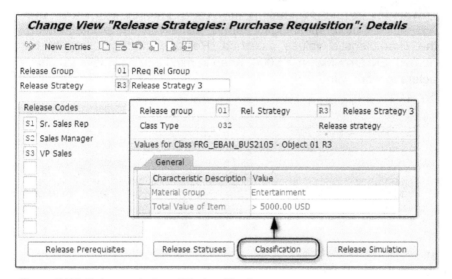

Figure 7.75: Release strategy R3 classification

Release Group	Release Strategy	Releases Required	Characteristic: Material Group	Characteristic: Requisition Value
01	R1	S1	Entertainment	< 500.00 USD
01	R2	S1 and S2	Entertainment	500.00 - 5000.00 USD
01	R3	S1, S2 and S3	Entertainment	> 5000.00 USD

Figure 7.76: Release strategy classification values

Finally, now that the prerequisites and the statuses have been config-ured, the classification section can be configured (see Figure 7.75). To see the settings for all three release strategies created, look at Figure 7.76. When you click on the CLASSIFICATION button, you will see the two characteristics listed. When you defined the material group characteris-tic, you enabled support for multiple entries; however, in the example you will only have the one material group, ENTERTAINMENT, listed. Release strategy R3 is the highest level in the group of strategies, so to obtain the TOTAL VALUE OF ITEM, you will want to catch all values that are greater than $5,000.

Release strategy naming convention

The example used a very poor naming convention by just naming the strategies 1, 2, and 3. See Figure 7.77 for how unhelpful the strategy name is as it is displayed on the purchase requisition. In practice, you should use more meaningful names, usually a name that reflects the characteristic values assigned. Release strategy 3 could be named, ENTERTAINMENT > 5000. Keep in mind you only have 20 char-acters to work with.

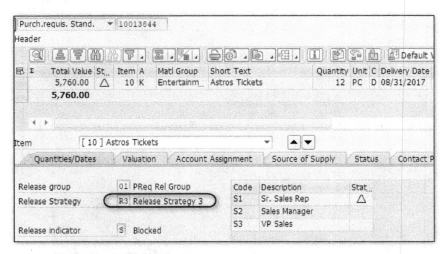

Figure 7.77: Example of requisition under release strategy

⑤ of Figure 7.68 shows where to assign organizational objects or SAP user IDs to release codes (see Figure 7.78). Notice the plant column. You can assign more than one organizational object or user to a release code based on the plant value of the requisition. The example does not show how to take advantage of the plant distinction functionality. You have assigned jobs that correspond to the Sr. Sales Rep, Sales Manager, and the VP of Sales. Whenever a requisition item has the material group ENTERTAINMENT, the requisition release work item will be sent to all the employees who have the job, Sr. Sales Rep. If the requisition value is over $500, once the Sr. Sales Rep has released the requisition, a work item will be sent to all the users who have the job assignment of Sales Manager. If the value is over $5,000, then in addition to the two previous releases, it will also be sent to all the users who have the job assignment of VP of Sales, which is most likely one person.

Alternative way to maintain release procedures

The release procedures are characteristics of class type 032, RELEASE STRATEGY, and can be viewed via transactions CL02. The characteristics of the class may be maintained via transaction CL24N.

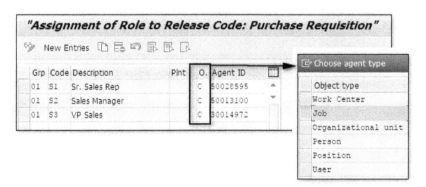

Figure 7.78: Assignment of organization object to release code

The scenario for the workshop will now change a little. Currently, all users who have the job as Sales Manager will receive the S2 release work item. Now, if there is a valid cost center or multiple cost centers assigned to the requisition item, you will program the release procedure user exit to send the approval to cost center manager(s). Before the value in view V_T16FW is overridden, the exit will make sure that the cost center owner has the appropriate release code authorization.

The first step for using the customer exit is to change the release code that will now be using the customer exit. In the example, change release code S2 to have a workflow setting of '9', for user exit (see Figure 7.79). Keep the assignment of the organization object to release code configuration in place, as shown in Figure 7.78, so it can be used as a fallback if the user exit does not find a valid approver. Note: You will have to program the user exit to read this configuration table to obtain the fallback value because once SAP hands the reigns over to the customer exit, SAP assumes the configuration will not be used.

So as a recap, release codes S1 and S3 will always be obtained by reading configuration values. S2 will use the customer exit to find agents and fall back on the configuration if none are found via the user exit.

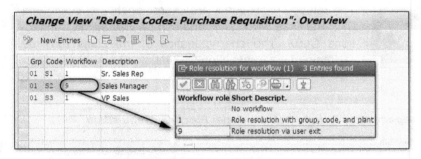

Figure 7.79: Release code configured to use user exit

Customer exit ZXM06U12, exit used to determine the agent of the requisition workflow:

SMOD Enhancement: M06B0001

Function module: EXIT_SAPLEBNF_001

▶ Create a CMOD project that includes SMOD enhancement, M06B001, which contains include ZXM06U12 that can be created and will be called from the customer exit function module EXIT_SAPLEBNF_001.

This exit will obtain the cost center information that was written to memory via a BAdI. An implementation of BAdI ME_PROCESS_REQ _CUST is created via transaction SE19. The exit will find the users responsible for these cost centers. If the cost center's responsible users have the authorization to release the requisition, they will be added to the list of possible agents. If they do not have authorization, the exit will fall back on reading the configuration to find the agents.

```
*&--------------------------------------------------------------*
*&  Include           ZXM06U12
*&  →include is inside of empty funtcion module
*&  EXIT_SAPLEBNF_001
*&--------------------------------------------------------------*
*FUNCTION EXIT_SAPLEBNF_001.
**"--------------------------------------------------------------
**"*"Lokale Schnittstelle:
**"        IMPORTING
**"             VALUE(I_EBAN) LIKE  EBAN STRUCTURE  EBAN
**"             VALUE(I_FRGCO) LIKE  T16FC-FRGCO
**"        TABLES
**"             ACTOR_TAB STRUCTURE  SWHACTOR
**"             AC_CONTAINER STRUCTURE  SWCONT
**"--------------------------------------------------------------
DATA: ls_actor TYPE swhactor.

* Get Cost Center Info - The cost center data is written to
* memory from from a requisition BAdI
* Classic BAdI: ME_PROCESS_REQ_CUST
* Method: IF_EX_ME_PROCESS_REQ_CUST~PROCESS_ACCOUNT
TYPES: BEGIN OF ty_cost_center,
         kokrs TYPE csks-kokrs,
         kostl TYPE csks-kostl,
       END OF ty_cost_center.
DATA: lt_cost_center TYPE TABLE OF ty_cost_center,
      ls_cost_center TYPE ty_cost_center.
CLEAR: lt_cost_center, ls_cost_center.
IMPORT lt_cost_center TO lt_cost_center
       FROM MEMORY ID 'REQ_KOSTL'.
```

```abap
* Read user responsible for any cost centers found and check
* that the cost center owner has release authorization required
DATA: lv_owner TYPE xubname.
LOOP AT lt_cost_center INTO ls_cost_center.
  SELECT SINGLE verak_user FROM csks
       INTO lv_owner
     WHERE kokrs = ls_cost_center-kokrs
       AND kostl = ls_cost_center-kostl.
  IF sy-subrc = 0.
    AUTHORITY-CHECK OBJECT 'M_BANF_FRG'
              FOR USER lv_owner
              ID 'FRGCD' FIELD i_frgco.
    IF sy-subrc = 0.
      ls_actor-otype = 'US'.
      ls_actor-objid = lv_owner.
      APPEND ls_actor TO actor_tab.
    ENDIF.
  ENDIF.
ENDLOOP.

* If no agent found or if Cost Center Ownwer does not have the
* release code authorization required then we will fall back
* to the organization object/user assignments configured
* for the release codes.
IF actor_tab[] IS INITIAL.
  SELECT SINGLE otype objid
           FROM t16fw
           INTO ( ls_actor-otype, ls_actor-objid )
          WHERE frggr = i_eban-frggr
            AND frgco = i_frgco.
  IF sy-subrc = 0.
    APPEND ls_actor TO actor_tab.
  ENDIF.
ENDIF.
```

8 Appendix

8.1 Agent tables

8.1.1 Work item recipients

Take a look behind the scenes at the tables that hold the possible agents and the recipients. As shown for the work item in Figure 8.1, the possible agents are shown—divided into the roles or organizational objects they are assigned to—once you click on the [Overall view] icon from the POSSIBLE AGENTS pop-up. When you are shown the possible agents, you can tell which are also recipients by the INBOX icon beside the agent's name.

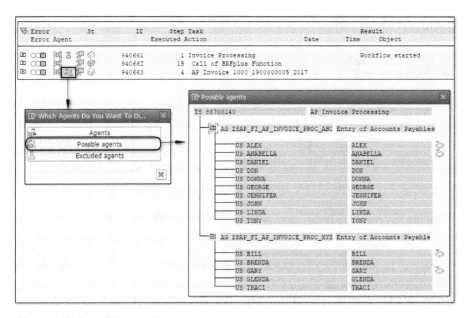

Figure 8.1: Possible agents

The HR relationship table HRP1001, as shown in Figure 8.2, holds the relationship records for the task's possible agents; all the organizational objects, or in this case, the roles the task is assigned to. The RELATION-

SHIP is always A with Relationship object 007 from the task to the organizational objects or roles.

	Search in Table	HRP1001		Infotype 1001 DB Table	
	Number of hits	2			
	Runtime	0		Maximum no. of hits	500

🔲	Ob	Object ID	Relationship	Relationship object	Rel.obj.type	ID of related object
	TS	88700140	A	007	AG	ZSAP_FI_AP_INVOICE_PROC_XYZ
	TS	88700140	A	007	AG	ZSAP_FI_AP_INVOICE_PROC_ABC

Figure 8.2: HR relationship table HRP1001

A task may not have any entries in table HRP1001; this will be the case if the task is set as a general task. Table HRP1217 holds the setting for GENERAL TASK (see Figure 8.3). This table holds many task attributes, in addition to the general task setting.

HRP1217: Display of Entries Found

🔲	PV	Ob	Object ID	Start date	End Date	Classification	General Task	No gen.forwarding	No Forward
	01	TS	88700145	04/30/2017	12/31/9999	2	X		
	01	TS	88700146	05/20/2017	07/14/2017	4		X	
	01	TS	88700151	08/18/2017	12/31/9999		X		
	01	WS	88700255	04/29/2017	12/31/9999		X		

Figure 8.3: Table HRP1217, general task setting

Tables SWWORGTASK and SWWUSERWI hold the recipients for each work item. Remember, recipients are defined as the intersection of possible agents and responsible agents while excluding the excluded agents. Table SWWORGTASK will hold the organizational objects of the work item recipients. Field ORG_OBJ is the concatenation of the 1- or 2-digit organizational object identifier plus the object ID, e.g. S for position and the position ID of 99182330 would have a value of S 99182330. Table SWWUSERWI holds the recipients resolved to SAP user IDs. If the task is a general task, tables SWWORGTASK and SWWUSERID will hold a record for each instantiated work item of this task, but field ORG_OBJ for table SWWORGTASK will be blank and field USER_ID for table SWWUSERID will be blank.

Figure 8.4 shows the agents, or recipients, of the task. You can see that all four recipients have the work item in their inboxes. This means the work item has not been executed or reserved by anyone. If you look at tables SWWORGTASK and SWWUSERWI for this work item, you see that none of the records has the IRRELEVANT flag set (see Figure 8.5).

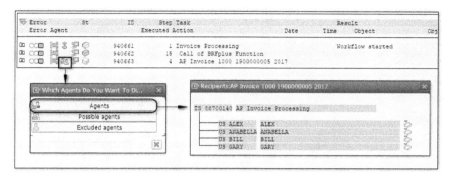

Figure 8.4: Recipients (agents)

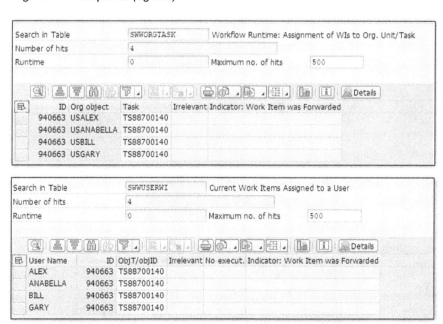

Figure 8.5: Tables SWWORGTASK and SWWUSERWI

Once user Anabella reserves the work item, the table entries now reflect that Alex, Bill, and Gary no longer have the work item visible in their in-boxes. You know this because the IRRELEVANT flag is marked for each, see Figure 8.6. If Anabella places the work item back into the queue, the IRRELEVANT flag will be removed from users Alex, Bill, and Gary again.

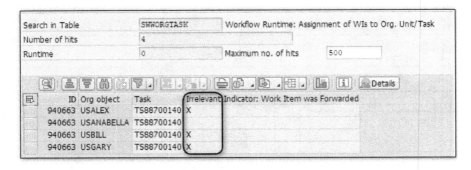

Search in Table	SWWORGTASK	Workflow Runtime: Assignment of WIs to Org. Unit/Task
Number of hits	4	
Runtime	0	Maximum no. of hits	500

	ID	Org object	Task	Irrelevant	Indicator: Work Item was Forwarded
	940663	USALEX	TS88700140	X	
	940663	USANABELLA	TS88700140		
	940663	USBILL	TS88700140	X	
	940663	USGARY	TS88700140	X	

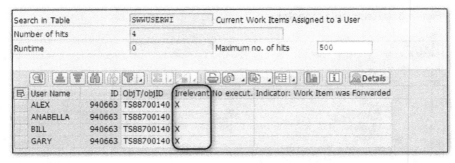

Search in Table	SWWUSERWI	Current Work Items Assigned to a User
Number of hits	4	
Runtime	0	Maximum no. of hits	500

User Name	ID	ObjT/objID	Irrelevant	No execut.	Indicator: Work Item was Forwarded
ALEX	940663	TS88700140	X		
ANABELLA	940663	TS88700140			
BILL	940663	TS88700140	X		
GARY	940663	TS88700140	X		

Figure 8.6: Irrelevant agents are not selected agents

You may wonder why tables SWWORGTASK and SWWUSERWI have identical entries. This is not always the case. Look at an example where there are possible agents defined, but the rule does not return any agents (see Figure 8.7). Because the rule does not return any responsible agents, the actual agents will turn out to be the possible agents defined.

Now look at tables SWWORGTASK and SWWUSERWI, as shown in Figure 8.8, and see how they are different. Table SWWORGTASK has an empty entry for the work item; this tells you the work item is for a task that is set as a general task. Table SWWUSERWI holds the users who are actual agents, possible agents, responsible agents, and not excluded agents. The table only holds SAP user IDs; all organizational objects and roles are resolved to SAP user IDs.

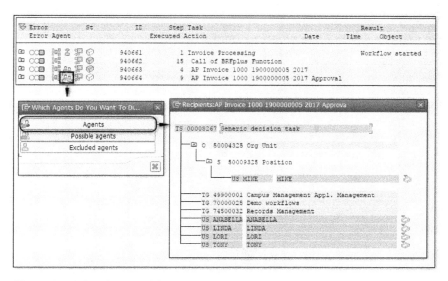

Figure 8.7: Work item recipients, agents

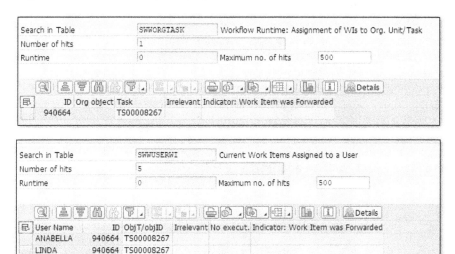

Figure 8.8: Tables SWWORGTASK and SWWUSERWI

Unlike table SWWUSERWI, which resolves all the agents to SAP user IDs, table HRP1001, as shown in Figure 8.9, shows the possible agents as the organizational objects or roles the users are assigned to. In this case, the possible agents of the task happen to be four SAP user IDs, but you can see the one organizational object as well.

Search in Table	HRP1001	Infotype 1001 DB Table	
Number of hits	5		
Runtime	0	Maximum no. of hits	500

Ob	Object ID	Relationship	Relationship object	Rel.obj.type	ID of related object
TS	8267	A	007	US	ANABELLA
TS	8267	A	007	US	LINDA
TS	8267	A	007	US	TONY
TS	8267	A	007	US	LORI
TS	8267	A	007	O	50004325

Figure 8.9: HR relationship table HRP1001

8.1.2 Excluded agents

Excluded agents are defined as container elements with a domain of HROBJEC_14. Organizational objects or SAP user IDs can be assigned to this container element with the 2-digit organizational object designation concatenated to the organizational object ID or SAP user ID.

Excluded agents are visible when you click on the agents' icon from the workflow log with an ✖ beside their name, see Figure 8.10. Excluded agents are resolved to SAP user IDs and stored in table SWWWIAGENT, see Figure 8.11, with an agent type of E for excluded.

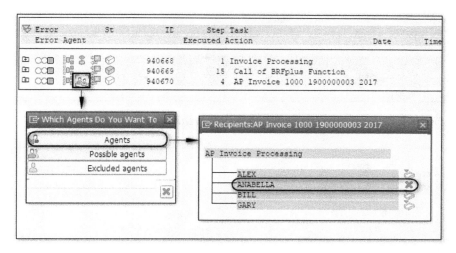

Figure 8.10: Excluded agent shown with ✖ in workflow log

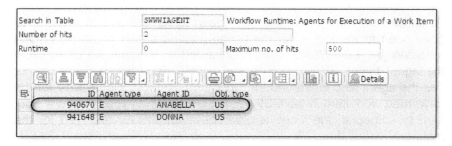

Figure 8.11: Table SWWWIAGENT

8.1.3 Forwarded agents

You may want to find work items that have been forwarded to someone else. Table SWWLOGHIST provides a way of finding forwarded work items and Figure 8.12 shows the associated workflow log. Figure 8.13 shows the corresponding entry in table SWWLOGHIST.

☞ Error	St	ID	Step Task			Result	
Error Agent			Executed Action	Date	Time	Object	Object Name
⊞ ○○▣ ▤▤ ⑇ ▦ ⌀		940668	1 Invoice Processing				Workflow started
⊞ ○○▣ ▤▤ ▦ ⊕		940669	15 Call of BRFplus Function				
▣ ○○▣ ▤▤ ▣ ⌀		940670	4 AP Invoice 1000 1900000003 2017				
○○▣ Workflow-System			Dialog work item created	09.10.2017	00:50:34		
○○▣ BILL			Work item reserved	15.10.2017	22:15:08		
○○▣ BILL			Work item forwarded	15.10.2017	22:15:08	Address...	LORI

Figure 8.12: Work item log, work item was forwarded

Search in Table	SWWLOGHIST	Workflow Runtime: History of a Work Item	
Number of hits	1		
Runtime	0	Maximum no. of hits	500

	ID	Action	End Date	End time	Agent	Object ID	
	940670	SWW_WI_FORWARD	10/15/2017	22:15:08	BILL	I68CLNT850ADDRESS	ORGUSLORI

Figure 8.13: SWWLOGHIST

To find all the work items that have been forwarded and to whom they have been forwarded, enter the action (technical field name METHOD) as SWW_WI_FORWARD. Note: Forwarded work items will show up in the agent tables SWWUSERWI and SWWORGTASK, but you cannot see the agent who forwarded the work item. Refer to Figure 8.14 for the forwarded work item in table SWWORGTASK. When you forward a work item to someone, the work item will be automatically reserved for the recipient.

SWWORGTASK: Display of Entries Found

Search in Table	SWWORGTASK	Workflow Runtime: Assignment of WIs to Org. Unit/Task	

	ID	Org object	Task	Irrelevant	Indicator: Work Item was Forwarded
	940670	USALEX	TS88700140	X	
	940670	USANABELLA	TS88700140	X	
	940670	USBILL	TS88700140	X	
	940670	USGARY	TS88700140	X	
	940670	USLORI	TS88700140		X

Figure 8.14: Table SWWORGTASK with forwarded work item

8.1.4   Substitutes

Personal substitutions

Table HRUS_D2 holds all the personal substitution records. Field US_NAME corresponds to the original agent, field REP_NAME corresponds to the substitute. The HRUS_D2 record will also show you begin and end dates of the substitution period; the classification profile, if one is used; and whether or not the substitution is for active or for passive substitution. Figure 8.15 shows several records from table HRUS_D2. From these records, you can see that both Anabella and Donna are substitutes of Bill. There was a temporary substitution of Donna for Bill for the month of April. Later in June, it was decided to make Donna a substitution for Bill until 12/31/9999. Anabella is a substitute for APPROVAL work items and Donna is a substitute for PROFESSIONAL work items. All three records are for active substitution as opposed to passive. Note that the record for Donna substituting for Bill which expires on 04/30/2017 is no longer valid, yet the active flag is still set; this does not make it active if the date is out of range, the active flag just means that this is not passive substitution.

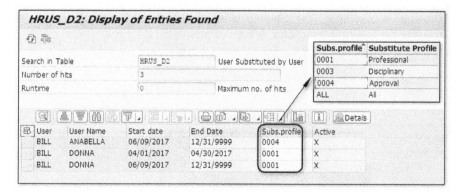

Figure 8.15: Table HRUS_D2

HR substitutes

The HR table HRP1001 holds all HR relationships, including substitute relationships. The substitute records all have the field RELAT, with the description, RELAT'SHIP equal to 210. All the records with RSIGN = 'A' will have the original agent as OTYPE / OBJID and the substitute as SCLAS / SOBID. The records with RSIGN = 'B' will show the substitute as OTYPE / OBJID and the original agent as SCLAS / SOBID. Figure 8.16 shows example substitution records.

HRP1001: Display of Entries Found

Search in Table — HRP1001 — Infotype 1001 DB Table

Ob	Object ID S	Relat'ship	Start date	End Date	RO	ID rel.object
S	50003807 B	210	01/01/2002	12/31/9999	S	50014740
S	50014740 A	210	01/01/2002	12/31/9999	S	50003807

Figure 8.16: HR relationship table, HRP1001

See ❶ in Figure 8.16 for the record that shows the top-down (RSIGN = 'B') relationship of position S50003807. This shows that the Audit Director, position S50003807, is a substitute for position S50014740. ❷ in Figure 8.16 shows the reverse bottom-up (RSIGN = 'A') entry. Using transaction po13, you can see all the relationships associated with position S50003807 (see Figure 8.17). The highlighted entry is the top-down entry shown at ❶ in Figure 8.16. Finally, Figure 8.18 is a view of Lori Rhodes' substitutes. You can see that Lori holds an auditor's position and she has the audit director, Mike, as a substitute.

Position — Dir. Audit — Audit Director (US)
Planning Status — Active
Relationships — 01 S 50003807 1

Start	End	R..	Rel...	Relat.text	R..	Rel'd obje...	Abbr.	% Rate
01/01/2002	12/31/9999	A	003	Belongs to	O	50028926	Int Audit-US	0.00
08/01/2002	12/31/9999	A	008	Holder	P	00100251	Horn	100.00
09/04/2017	12/31/9999	B	007	Is describ	TG	88700002	zAudit	0.00
01/01/2002	12/31/9999	B	210	Substitute	S	50014740	Auditor	0.00

Figure 8.17: Position substitution

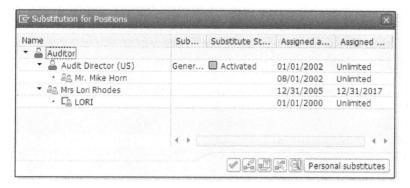

Figure 8.18: Transaction RMPS_SET_SUBSTITUTE

8.2 Workflow agent transactions

Configuration
    OOAW Evaluation paths 55, 57, 106, 130
    OONR Number assignment 52
    OOW4 Prefix numbers for workflow and organizational management 52
    SWLV Maintain view 106
    SWU3 Automatic workflow customizing 38, 146
Customer Modifications
    CMOD Project Management of SAP Enhancements 226
    SE19 BAdI Builder 227
Master data
    CL02 Maintain class 225
    CL24N Assign objects/classes to class 225
    OOCU_RESP Maintain responsibilities 54
    PFOM Assignment to SAP organizational objects 61
    PO01 Maintain work center 129
    PO11 Maintain qualification 55
    PO13 Maintain position 238
    PPOM Organization and staffing (workflow) 28, 60
    RMPS_SET_SUBSTITUTE Define substitute (admin) 160, 239
    SO15 or SO23 Maintain distribution lists 98
    SU3 Maintain parameter IDs 170
Object definition
    BRF+ Business Rule Framework workbench 68
    PFAC Maintain rule 43, 50, 57, 58, 162, 192

You have finished the book.

A The Author

Gretchen Horn, previously Gretchen Roberts, received a bachelor's degree in Management Information Systems from the University of Houston. She has worked with SAP software since 1996 when she was an employee of Schlumberger Oilfield Services, working as a materials management functional subject matter expert. She became a consultant for N2 Consulting Inc. in 1998 so that she could focus on workflow design and development as a technical consultant. She is certified in SAP Business Workflow and in 2009, she began her own company, JLM Workflow Inc. She enjoys consulting locally in Houston, Texas.

B Index

C Disclaimer

This publication contains references to the products of SAP SE.

SAP, R/3, SAP NetWeaver, Duet, PartnerEdge, ByDesign, SAP BusinessObjects Explorer, StreamWork, and other SAP products and services mentioned herein as well as their respective logos are trademarks or registered trademarks of SAP SE in Germany and other countries.

Business Objects and the Business Objects logo, BusinessObjects, Crystal Reports, Crystal Decisions, Web Intelligence, Xcelsius, and other Business Objects products and services mentioned herein as well as their respective logos are trademarks or registered trademarks of Business Objects Software Ltd. Business Objects is an SAP company.

Sybase and Adaptive Server, iAnywhere, Sybase 365, SQL Anywhere, and other Sybase products and services mentioned herein as well as their respective logos are trademarks or registered trademarks of Sybase, Inc. Sybase is an SAP company.

SAP SE is neither the author nor the publisher of this publication and is not responsible for its content. SAP Group shall not be liable for errors or omissions with respect to the materials. The only warranties for SAP Group products and services are those that are set forth in the express warranty statements accompanying such products and services, if any. Nothing herein should be construed as constituting an additional warranty.

More Espresso Tutorials Books

Michal Krawczyk:

SAP® SOA Integration – Enterprise Service Monitoring

▶ Tools for Monitoring SOA Scenarios

▶ Forward Error Handling (FEH) and Error Conflict Handler (ECH)

▶ Configuration Tips

▶ SAP Application Interface Framework (AIF) Customization Best Practices

▶ Detailed Message Monitoring and Reprocessing Examples

http://5077.espresso-tutorials.com

Thomas Stutenbäumer:

Practical Guide to ABAP®. Part 1: Conceptual Design, Development, Debugging

▶ How to get the most out of SAP ABAP

▶ Guide for understanding and using the SAP Data Dictionary

▶ Beginner and advanced debugging techniques

▶ Expert ABAP development techniques

http://5121.espresso-tutorials.com

Anurag Barua:

First Steps in SAP® Fiori

- ► SAP Fiori fundamentals and core components
- ► Instructions on how to create and enhance an SAP Fiori app
- ► Installation and configuration best practices
- ► Similarities and differences between SAP Fiori and Screen Personas

http://5126.espresso-tutorials.com

Paul Bakker & Rick Bakker:

How to Pass the SAP® ABAP Certification Exam

- ► Essential guide on how to pass the ABAP Associate Certification exam
- ► Expert ABAP certification tips
- ► Overview of certification exam topics
- ► Short and full-length practice exams with answer guides

http://5136.espresso-tutorials.com

Thomas Stutenbäumer:

Practical Guide to ABAP®. Part 2: Performance, Enhancements, Transports

- ► Developer influence on performance
- ► Modifications and enhancements to SAP standard
- ► SAP access and account management techniques
- ► SAP Transport Management System

http://5138.espresso-tutorials.com

Prem Manghnani, Seshu Reddy & Sheshank Vyas:

Practical Guide to SAP® OpenUI5

- ▶ Fundamental OpenUI5 concepts
- ▶ How to define controls for an application
- ▶ SAP Fiori applications and design principles
- ▶ Real-world examples of how to create applications using

http://5148.espresso-tutorials.com

Raquel Seville:

SAP® OpenUI5 for Mobile BI and Analytics

- ▶ Delve into the foundations of CSS, HTML5, and jQuery
- ▶ Learn how to build a seamless mobile BI app using SAP OpenUI5
- ▶ Use open source library d3.js to create custom data visualizations for bar, line, and pie charts
- ▶ Build web apps using real world scenarios and test layout options for different mobile devices

http://5173.espresso-tutorials.com

Robert Burdwell:

First Steps for Building SAP®UI5 Mobile Apps

- ▶ Introduction to mobile and SAP UI5 development
- ▶ Steps for building mobile apps in Eclipse, SAP Cloud Platform, and Microsoft Visual Studio
- ▶ How to deploy apps to multiple devices
- ▶ Advantages and disadvantages of using different environments

http://5176.espresso-tutorials.com